10 Minute Guide to

Microsoft® Internet Explorer

by J. Michael Roach

que®

A Division of Macmillan Computer Publishing
201 West 103rd St., Indianapolis, Indiana 46290 USA

International Standard Book Number: 0-7897-0628-8
Library of Congress Catalog Card Number: 95-71044

97 96 95 3 2 1

Interpretation of the printing code: the rightmost number of the first series of numbers is the year of the book's printing; the rightmost number of the second series of numbers is the number of the book's printing. For example, a printing code of 95-1 shows that the first printing of the book occurred in 1995.

Screen reproductions in this book were created by means of the program Collage Plus from Inner Media, Inc., Hollis, NH.

Printed in the United States of America

President Roland Elgey

Publisher Stacy Hiquet

Publishing Director Brad R. Koch

Editorial Services Director Elizabeth Keaffaber

Managing Editor Sandy Doell

Director of Marketing Lynn E. Zingraf

Senior Series Editor Chris Nelson

Acquisitions Editor Beverly M. Eppink

Product Director Benjamin Milstead

Production Editor Danielle Bird

Copy Editor Charles K. Bowles II

Technical Advisors Jeff Bankston, Peter Kent

Figure Specialist Cari Skaggs

Book Designer Kim Scott

Cover Designer Dan Armstrong

Operations Coordinator Patricia J. Brooks

Editorial Assistant Andrea Duvall

Acquisitions Coordinator Ruth Slates

Production Team Angela Bannan, Becky Beheler, Chad Dressler, Maxine Dillingham, Joan Evan, Jason Hand, Darren Jackson, Damon Jordan, Paige Kane, Clint Lahnen, Laura Robbins, Bobbi Satterfield, Craig Small, Michael Thomas, Scott Tullis, and Todd Wente

Indexer Kathy Venable

J. Michael Roach, a native of St. Louis, MO, now lives in Columbia, MO where he works as a teacher, trainer, and course developer for DATASTORM, publisher of the award-winning PROCOMM PLUS line of communications software.

J. Michael started working with the Internet about a year and a half ago, and helped develop the company-wide Internet training for DATASTORM. Since that time, he has shared his enthusiasm for the Internet with friends, family, and colleagues. The *10 Minute Guide to Microsoft Internet Explorer* is his second Internet-related project with Que. He also wrote the *10 Minute Guide to Internet Assistant for Word.*

Contents

Introduction

Well, here we are, halfway through the last decade of the twentieth century, and an awful lot has happened so far. We've seen Microsoft rise to the top of the personal computing industry, the Internet has caused a technology explosion—even in Hollywood, and Microsoft has just completed one of the biggest products launched in the history of personal computing: Windows 95.

So, the year 2000 approaches, and there's still a lot left to happen in this millennium. We'll see the Internet and personal computing become an integral part of most people's daily lives. For that reason, I'd like to congratulate you for becoming a part of the computing world at this exciting point in computing history.

Businesses, colleges, universities, and private individuals are using the Internet for pleasure, entertainment, information, research, and financial gain—and so can you. With Windows 95 comes an improved, easier-than-ever-to-use interface. And tools that let you connect to the Internet automatically if you have a modem. It's so easy, it's almost scary.

This book concentrates on using Internet Explorer, a program available from Microsoft, to use the Internet and the World Wide Web. If you're new to all of this or you'd like more general information on the Internet, consider reading the *10 Minute Guide to the Internet* or the *10 Minute Guide to Using the Internet with Windows 95*.

Welcome to the *10 Minute Guide to Microsoft Internet Explorer*

Because most people don't have the time to sit down for a few consecutive hours, this book focuses on the fundamentals of using Microsoft Internet Explorer (you will not learn everything about the program). You can learn each feature or concept in a single lesson that takes 10 minutes or less to complete.

Straightforward, easy-to-follow explanations and numbered lessons get you up and running with Internet Explorer quickly by teaching by example. You'll see step-by-step directions that tell you exactly what to type, where to click, what keys to press—how to be productive with Internet Explorer right now.

WHO SHOULD USE THE *10 MINUTE GUIDE TO MICROSOFT INTERNET EXPLORER*

The 10 Minute Guide to Microsoft Internet Explorer is for anyone who:

- Needs to learn Internet Explorer quickly.
- Feels overwhelmed by the complexity of Internet Explorer or the Internet.
- Wants to find out quickly whether Internet Explorer will meet his or her needs.
- Wants a clear, concise guide to the most important features of Internet Explorer.

WHAT IS INTERNET EXPLORER?

Internet Explorer is a Web browser. What's a Web browser? A Web browser is a small utility that lets you look at documents on the Internet, save them, print them, or move on to another document. With a Web browser, using the Internet is as simple as point-and-click with your mouse.

Additionally, Internet Explorer has special features that allow you to use the powerful new features of Windows 95 to enhance your productivity on the Internet. Specifically:

- Support for built-in shortcuts; the ability to quickly and easily share information with other applications that surpasses the functionality of NetScape and other Web browsers.

- An easy-to-use interface.
- Quick right-click support for many of the most common features without having to find the command in a menu.

With these new features, your Web browsing experience will be more fun and more productive than it has in the past.

How to Use This Book

The 10 Minute Guide to Microsoft Internet Explorer consists of a series of lessons, ranging from basic startup to a few more advanced features.

If you've never used the Internet before, start with Lesson 1 and work forward at your own pace. If you're familiar with the Internet, you may feel comfortable skipping the first few lessons. The last few lessons deal with advanced features and give the advanced user an opportunity to become more familiar with Internet Explorer on a technical level.

Although you can use this book as a tutorial, it will also serve as a handy reference tool even after you become familiar with using Internet Explorer. Refer to this book if you forget how to perform a certain task or if the Help file doesn't contain a thorough reference.

Icons and Conventions Used in This Book

The following icons have been added throughout the book to help you find your way around:

> TIP **Timesaver Tip icons** offer shortcuts and hints for using the program efficiently.

Plain English icons define new terms.

Panic Button icons appear where new users often run into trouble.

The following conventions clarify the steps you perform:

On-screen text	Any text that appears on-screen appears in bold type.
What you type	The information you type appears in bold color type.
Press Enter	Keys you press (or selections you make with the mouse) appear in color type.
New terms	Any new terms appear in color type.
URLs	Addresses appear in bold color type.
Key+Key	When you need to use a two-key combination to enter a command (for example, "Alt+X"), press and hold the first key, and then tap the second key.

ACKNOWLEDGMENTS

I'd like to offer thanks to Beverly, who showed impeccable kindness and professionalism under normally high pressure conditions; you've made this project run very smoothly.

Special thanks go to Peter Kent who wrote the chapter on shopping.

I'd also like to offer thanks to John Dupuy, a notable author in his own right, who helped with a lot of last-minute information and clarification.

Thanks go out to my father, who refused to think the Internet was cool until he found the Formula I racing statistics online.

I'd like to extend my heartfelt thanks to Benjamin Milstead, whose feverish help and calm patience made this book possible in a truly adventurous deadline.

And finally, special thanks to Gary and Nelly—I can go to happy hour now, the book is done!

Trademarks

Understanding the Internet and the Web

LESSON 1

In this lesson, you'll learn about the Internet and the World Wide Web, including a bit of their histories.

Understanding the Internet

The Internet is a vast, worldwide network of millions of computers. Fast and powerful, the Net now contains more information than is available in all the world's libraries.

Who uses the Net? All kinds of people, most of them just like you. If you spend any time online, you'll meet:

- Students and faculty of large universities and small colleges.
- Senators, Representatives, and other local, state, and federal government officials. Even the President of the United States!
- Employees and owners of corporations, large and small. Microsoft, IBM, Intel, and DATASTORM are among the many computer companies you'll find on the Internet.
- Private individuals from all walks of life who use their local Internet service provider—and the established memberships of Prodigy, America Online, CompuServe, and thousands of BBS services.

The Internet uses the phone system to carry information from one place to another; how you connect your computer to the phone system depends to some extent on your location, but mostly on how much you can afford. Three major on-ramps to the Net now exist:

- The modem, which converts digital information to sound, transmits data at a number of different speeds. In just a few years modems have moved from speeds of 300 and 2400 to 14,400 bps—and even 28,800 bps is now affordable.
- Special copper phone lines, called ISDN (for Interactive Digital Services Network), handle speeds of up to 56k (56,000 bytes per second).
- Fiber optic cables, called T1 and T3 lines, carry lots of information over long distances. Used mainly by universities and large corporations, they are the major backbones of the Net.

The Internet is the only example of anarchy that works; by simple mutual agreement, millions of people share a common goal: communication and ideas flourish when people all over the world use the fastest and most powerful method for interaction.

The Internet offers a variety of ways for people to communicate and interact. Spend an hour or two hooked up and you'll discover:

- Telnet Terminal Emulation Link NETwork. Telnet allows you to connect to a remote system and operate it from your computer. Since Internet Explorer doesn't support the use of telnet, I won't discuss it in this book.
- FTP File Transfer Protocol. This service allows you to connect to another computer and to transfer files from that computer to your own. You can also transfer files from your computer to the other. I'll show you how to use FTP with Internet Explorer in Lesson 14.

- gopher Named for the mascot at the University of Minnesota (where gopher was developed), gopher allows you to connect to a machine that houses menus of information. The World Wide Web was developed from ideas and technology first used in gopher. Lesson 13 shows you how to use gopher with Internet Explorer.
- WWW World Wide Web. A complex collection of electronic documents scattered throughout the Internet. Each of these documents "points" to other documents on the Web. I'll explain how this works in the next section.
- e-mail Electronic mail is a method of sending and receiving typed notes or letters across a computer network. Most large corporations have some sort of internal e-mail capability. The Internet gives anyone connected that same capability. Although Internet Explorer only supports the capability to send e-mail (you can't receive), I'll show you how to do that in Lesson 16.
- UseNet A collection of discussion groups or newsgroups. These messages (usually stored in several central locations or news servers), are similar to those found on a BBS, or a CompuServe forum, or the bulletin board in the office break room. Users can read items from other users, or post questions or comments of their own. Often, UseNet newsgroups are a place for experts within a field to "gather" and discuss current trends and such. Researchers and scientists working on similar projects also use UseNet to share information. Internet Explorer does not support UseNet.

Internet Explorer is designed to use the World Wide Web, so I'll concentrate on that in the next section. If you'd like to learn more about the others, consider reading Que's *10 Minute Guide to the Internet,* or if you're fairly experienced with computers, check out *Special Edition Using the Internet,* also published by Que.

UNDERSTANDING THE WEB

The World Wide Web is a large collection of documents stored on the Internet. Each of these documents "points" to other documents on the Internet through the use of a technology called HyperText Transfer Protocol, (HTTP for short). If you're not familiar with hypertext, it's very simple to explain: if you've ever used a Windows Help file, you'll remember those little highlighted words that, when you click on them, bring up a page of information related to the word you clicked on.

Now, if the preceding paragraph were written using hypertext, I would have created a link to a page that gave a definition for the word "hypertext," and programmed that link to that word in the above paragraph. That way, when you clicked on "hypertext," you'd see the definition. I'll show you how it works in Lesson 3.

To understand hypertext is to understand the possibilities of the World Wide Web. When you look at a document, you can jump to other documents on the Web with related (or sometimes nonrelated) information. Those documents also point to other documents. Surfing the Net—or browsing through document after document on the World Wide Web—has turned a mouse-click into a key that opens up endless treasure chests of information on the Net.

Well, in order to browse the Web or surf the Net, you'll need a Web browser such as Internet Explorer. A Web browser is a piece of computer software that request documents (or Web pages) from the Internet and puts them on-screen so you can see them. How does this work?

Each document is identified by a Uniform Resource Locator or URL (pronounced "earl" or "U-R-L"). The URL contains three important pieces of information:

- The protocol used to transfer the information. A protocol, in general, is a list of rules or steps used to accomplish or perform a task. Ambassadors use a protocol to determine how to respond in certain international situations. Computers use protocols to determine how to transfer data from one machine to another. Think of a protocol as a language that computers use to talk to one another.

- The domain name of the machine on the Internet that contains the document. A domain name is a naming scheme used by the Internet to allow humans to easily identify a specific computer. Each domain name represents a numerical address. The domain name is translated in the numerical address (which the computer needs) by a Domain Name Server (or DNS). The DNS translates a domain name into a numerical address known as an IP address. Every computer on the Internet has its own unique IP address that distinguishes it from other machines. An IP address is a numerical representation of a 32-bit addressing structure used by the Internet. An IP address might look something like this: 11001101100010101011111100001110. Wow! That's a lot to remember. We can convert this number into something more understandable: 205.138.191.14. But even that's difficult to remember. That's why the DNS is used. Instead of that nasty number, we can use michaelr.datastorm.com. It's easier to remember "Michael's machine at DATASTORM" this way. This text equivalent is called the alias of the IP address.
- The path and filename to that document

The World Wide Web uses HTTP to transfer Web pages from one machine to another. By convention, we use :// after the name of the protocol. So, the first part of an URL might look like:

http://

Now, we can put the first two parts of our URL together:

http://michaelr.datastorm.com

This tells us:

- Use HTTP to transfer this document
- Go to Michael's machine at DATASTORM to find the document.

We also need to tell the server which document we want.

> **Server** A computer on the Internet that stores information and documents. Each server runs a program (also called a server) that waits for requests for this information. A server that stores Web pages is called a Web server or Web site.

We can request a specific document from the server, as well. In the above example, we did not specify a document, so we would get the Home Page from that server (someone set that up at the remote system, so, luckily, we don't have to worry about it).

> **Home Page** Home Page refers to the main document you see when you first connect to a Web server. This page is also referred to as a Start Page.

Let's look at this URL:

http://michaelr.datastorm.com/documents/books/QUE/InternetExplorer.html

This URL tells the server to look in the /documents/books/QUE directory and get the file called InternetExplorer.html. Most HTML files will end in .htm or .html.

> **HTML** HyperText Markup Language. This is a text-based editing language used to create the documents you see on the World Wide Web. For more information about HTML and how to create your own documents, consider reading the *10 Minute Guide to Internet Assistant for Word* or the *10 Minute Guide to HTML.*

Besides the test itself, the people who create HTML for you to view use a number of different technologies to allow multimedia over the Internet. You'll find these things in the documents you view:

- Pictures The author can also put pictures in a Web page. These are known as inline graphics. By inline graphic, I mean a graphic that appears as part of the document instead of in another window.
- HyperLinks You'll find hypertext links not only to other documents, but also to sound files, motion video files, graphics, photos, and other multimedia files. Most browsers nowadays have the capability to play sound files and various types of animations. And, if they don't, you can configure an external program to do it instead. We'll have to do this, since Internet Explorer doesn't play sound or animation. I'll explain how in Lesson 19.
- Forms Forms give you the capability to communicate with the server and to send back information. You can use forms to register software, request information, search for information, and even order pizza.

In this lesson, you learned about the Internet and the World Wide Web. In the next lesson, you'll learn how to start and exit Internet Explorer, and how to get online Help.

Lesson 2: Exploring the Internet Explorer

In this lesson, you'll learn how to start and exit Internet Explorer. You'll also learn how to access Internet Explorer's online Help system.

What Is Internet Explorer?

Internet Explorer is a Web browser, a piece of computer software that requests Web pages from a Web server and displays them on-screen for you to read. However, there's more to it than that. Most modern Web browsers allow you to view gopher menus and to transfer files.

You can do all of these using a simple, straightforward, easy-to-use graphical interface. The ease-of-use of graphical interfaces has caused the single largest explosion in computer technology in a long time (if not the largest ever). Most of the time, you can't watch TV for more than five minutes without hearing some sort of reference to the Internet or the World Wide Web.

Since Microsoft introduced Windows, there has been a steady increase in the usability of computers by nontechnical people. Since the user can see an icon or visual representation of what he or she wants to accomplish, then click on it with the mouse, users no longer have to memorize complicated commands. Nor do they have to be skilled typists to be productive.

The Internet brought with it thousands of nasty, complicated, and hard-to-remember commands to type. When the World Wide Web brought the mouse into play, allowing a user to click his or her way through, nontechnical users finally had access to the Internet.

STARTING INTERNET EXPLORER

Internet Explorer is a part of the Microsoft Plus! Pack for Windows 95. If you haven't already installed the Plus! Pack, consult Appendix C, where I help you to install Internet Explorer. If you're ready to go with a fully installed version of Internet Explorer, let's proceed.

Windows 95 gives you a new and improved interface for operating your computer. Because of this new interface, you'll find that there is often more than one way to accomplish a specific task. This is a plus for you because you will be able to do more with less learning, and the learning you'll have to do will be much easier. Since there is more than one way to start Internet Explorer, I'll give you several options and you can use whichever method you like best.

First, you'll notice an Internet Explorer icon on your desktop, as shown in Figure 2.1.

FIGURE 2.1 The Internet Explorer icon.

Double-click this icon to start Internet Explorer. If you're using Internet Explorer with a modem, you may have to wait a few moments while Windows 95 dials into your Internet Service Provider. You'll see the screen shown in Figure 2.2, which is the main Internet Explorer window. Inside this window, you'll see the Start Page. The Start Page helps to get you started on the Internet.

FIGURE 2.2 The Internet Explorer main window. Microsoft changes this regularly, so you may see something different.

I Don't See Anything! If you don't see anything, there could be several problems. First, your Internet connection might not be working. If you're connecting to the Internet over a network, contact your system administrator to ensure that the network is working properly. If you're using the Internet over a modem, contact your Internet Service Provider for help.

Most of the work you'll do in Internet Explorer can be done from this main screen.

Exiting Internet Explorer

Once you've started Internet Explorer, you'll be able to browse the Web and gather information. After you're done browsing the Internet for the day, though, you'll likely want to shut down the program.

There are, however, a couple of things you should keep in mind when using applications under Windows 95:

- Windows 95 can run more than one application at a time, so you don't need to shut it down every time you want to do something else with your computer.
- Switching to another program does not stop the current program from running. If you're trying to load a page that takes a long time, you can switch to another program and Internet Explorer will load the page while you're working in the other program.

As in most other areas, Windows 95 offers several different methods for closing a program. You can use any of the following methods to exit Internet Explorer:

- Click the Exit button at the top right-hand corner of the Internet Explorer window.
- Open the system menu at the top left-hand corner and select the Close command.
- Open the File menu and select the Exit command.

Accessing the Help System

Windows 95 also boasts a new and improved Help system. This new system makes learning a new application easy and (dare I say?) fun.

To access the Help system, you can either:

- Press the F1 key at the top of your keyboard, or
- Open the Help item on the menu bar and select the Help Topics command.

You'll see the main Help screen.

> TIP **Help Is on Your Hard Drive** Unlike Netscape, Internet Explorer installs the help system on your hard drive. Most of the help information for Netscape is on the Internet, not on your computer. With Internet Explorer, you can still get help if the Microsoft server isn't working.

As in Windows 3.1, Windows 95 gives you two different methods for getting the help you need:

- A menu list of help topics cleverly arranged
- A search engine that allows you to type in a keyword, such as **URL**

I'll show you how to use both of these methods, and give you examples to help you learn.

Browsing the Help Topics

By default, you'll see a short list of main topics. Each of these topics has a book icon in front of it. Double-click the book to reveal the subtopics underneath (see Fig. 2.3). Notice that the book icon changed to an open book.

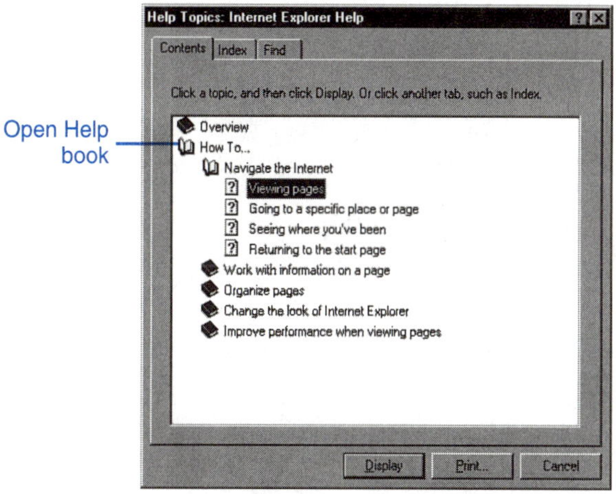

FIGURE 2.3 An open Help topics book.

Let's browse through a sample Help topic to give you a general idea of how it all works:

1. Open the Help menu and select the Help Topics command. You should see the main Help screen.
2. Double-click the How To... book. You should see the open How To... book as shown in Figure 2.3.
3. Double-click the Navigate the Internet book. You should see a list of topics underneath it, now. Note the Help topics have an icon with a piece of paper with a question mark inside.
4. Double-click the Viewing Pages topic. The Help window will disappear, and you'll see the Help Topic window, as shown in Figure 2.4.

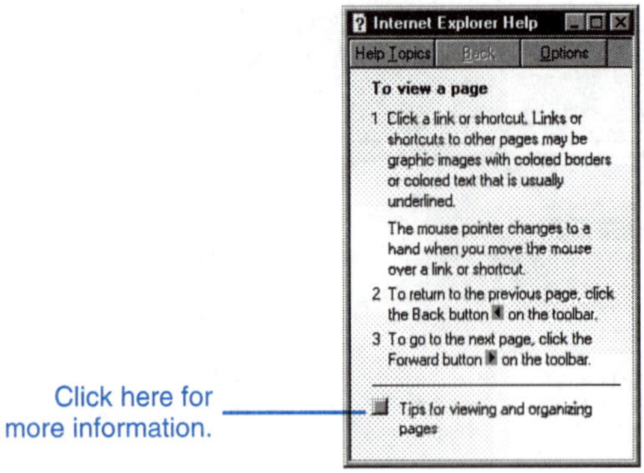

FIGURE 2.4 A sample topic window.

SEARCHING HELP FOR A SPECIFIC TOPIC

If you'd rather just get a bit of information on a specific topic, you can search for the lessons that relate to that topic. Let's use the same example as above to illustrate the point that you can use two methods to find information in the Help system. To search for information on viewing Web pages:

1. Open the Help menu and select the Help topics command. You should see the main Help screen.
2. Click the Index tab at the top of the window. You should see a window similar to that in Figure 2.5.
3. In the edit field under item 1, type the word **view**. The list should jump down to the topics that begin with the word "view," as shown in Figure 2.5.
4. To display the Help topic, click Display.

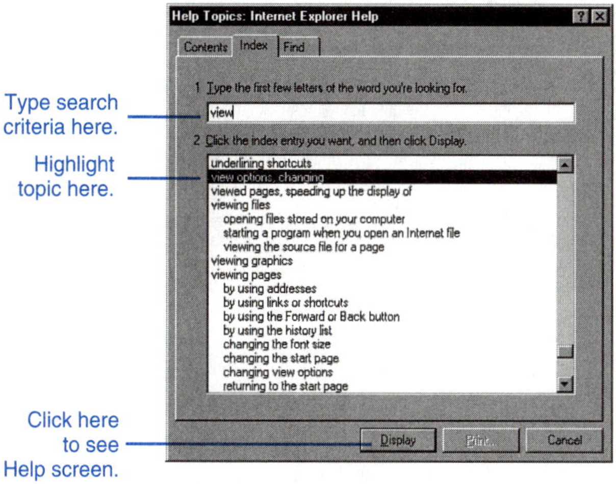

FIGURE 2.5 The Help Index window.

In this lesson, you learned how to start and exit Internet Explorer. You also learned how to access the online Help system.

In the next lesson, you'll learn how to get to your first Web page. You'll also learn how use hypertext to browse through the millions of documents on the Internet.

LESSON 3

GETTING STARTED WITH INTERNET EXPLORER

In this lesson, you'll learn how to get to your first Web page and how to use hypertext to browse through the millions of documents on the Internet. You'll also learn how to use the basic toolbar buttons.

UNDERSTANDING THE HOME PAGE

After you've started Internet Explorer (see Lesson 2 if you don't know how), you'll see the home page Microsoft has provided for you. This page exists on a computer at Microsoft.

Although it might not clear right away, the picture you see has hypertext capabilities, too. Each of the icons in the picture will take you to a new page. Feel free to browse.

If you want to use a different page as your starting point, see Lesson 21 for information on configuring advanced options in Internet Explorer.

LOADING A WEB PAGE

If you know the URL of the document you wish to see, you can use two methods to retrieve that document. The first method uses the toolbar or the menu bar:

1. Open the File item in the menu bar and select the Open command. You will see the Open Internet Address dialog box shown in Figure 3.1.

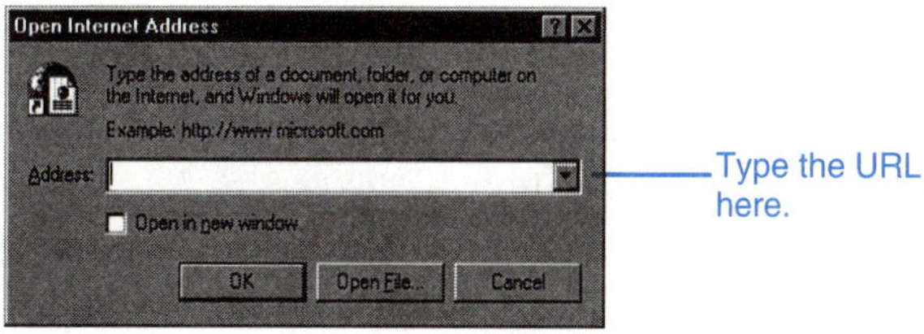

FIGURE 3.1 The Open Internet Address dialog box.

2. Type the URL in the space labeled Address: and click OK (or press Enter).
3. After a few moments (depending upon the speed of your connection), the document you wish to see will appear in the Internet Explorer window.

If you only need to view documents this way every once in a while, the above is the best way to do it. If, however, you find that you're typing URLs in all the time, there is an easier way:

1. Underneath your toolbar you will see a long, white field.
2. Highlight the text in that field and press the Delete key. The field will be empty now.
3. Type in the URL of the document you wish to see and press Enter.

Use whichever of the above two methods best suits your style. If you're a beginner and you're not sure which one is for you, use them both, and you'll eventually find the one that makes you feel most comfortable.

USING HYPERTEXT TO SURF THE NET

Great! Here we are. The single most important section in the whole book. And, you're in luck! It's the easiest, too.

The profound simplicity of the World Wide Web comes from a technology called hypertext. If you read Lesson 2, you'll remember my reference to a Windows Help file and the little highlighted words you see on each "page" of help. Well, the World Wide Web works the same way. Let's browse to a sample page and demonstrate hypertext.

1. Using one of two methods above (your choice), type:

   http://www.yahoo.com

   Press Enter. After a few moments, you will see the Yahoo home page, as shown in Figure 3.2.

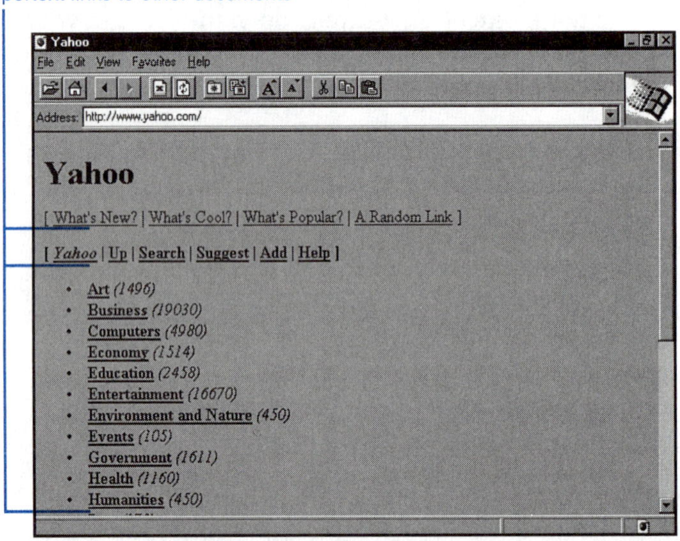

FIGURE 3.2 The Yahoo home page.

2. Each of the words in blue is a hyperlink to another page containing information related to the word itself. To continue this example, look for Computers in the list, and click it. *You need to click a hyperlink only once, not twice.*

3. Internet Explorer will then retrieve the Computers list. If you look at picture of the Microsoft Windows logo at the top right-hand corner, you'll notice that it looks like it's flying (the sky in the background moves) whenever Internet Explorer is retrieving (downloading) a document for you.
4. After the list of Computers topics is complete, look for a subtopic called Internet. Click the word Internet (remember: once, not twice).
5. The next list will be topics regarding the Internet. From here, choose whichever topic interests you the most.

You'll probably notice that you'd like to choose more than one. Internet Explorer allows you to view a page, then "go back" to the previous page to choose a different link. I'll explain that more in the next section.

You'll also notice that once you select the next page, another topic sounds interesting to you, as well. After you choose that one, yet another topic will intrigue you. So you choose it. After a few minutes, you might not be reading about the Internet at all anymore. This process is known as surfing the Net. Be careful. This is highly addicting, and a whole lot of fun! But don't worry, it's fat free, calorie free, and does not cause cancer.

Using the Toolbar to Surf the Net

In order to make your surfing more productive, Microsoft has provided a toolbar near the top of the window. This toolbar contains buttons that provide one-click access to the most common functions used in Internet Explorer. In this section, I'll cover the first six buttons. For information on the remaining buttons, see Lesson 4.

First, let's get familiar with the first six buttons on the toolbar:

BUTTON	NAME	FUNCTION
	Open URL	Open Internet Address (URL)
	Open Start Page	Open Start Page
	Back	Go back to the previous Web page.
	Forward	Go forward to the next Web page. *This works only after you've gone back to a previous page.*
	Stop	Stop current action in progress
	Refresh	Refresh or reload the current document

I'll address each button in its own section.

Using the Open URL Button

The Open button is the first button in your toolbar. This button performs the same function as the Open command in the File menu.

Using the Open Start Page Button

The Open Start Page button is the second button on your toolbar. By default, the Start page is the Microsoft Web server. To come back to this page from any point on the Internet, click the Open Start Page button.

Of course, you can change the Start Page to suit your own needs. For more information, see Lesson 21.

Using the Back and Forward Buttons

The Back and Forward buttons are the third and fourth buttons on your toolbar. These buttons are very helpful and useful when you are viewing pages that contain lots of information you want to see. Often, the home page at that site will contain links to most of the stuff you want to see; the easiest thing to do is to follow the links one at a time, and then use the Back button to retrace your steps. If you accidentally go back too far, use the Forward button to "undo" your "go back."

Here's an example:

1. Open the File menu and select the Open command. You will see the Open Internet Address dialog box.
2. Type **http://www.microsoft.com** and press Enter. After a few moments, you will see the Microsoft home page. Toward the bottom of this page (you may need to use the scroll bar at the right-hand side to view the rest of the document), you will see eight hyperlink choices.
3. Click Visit Microsoft. After a few moments, you will see the Microsoft Corporation Information page. But, let's pretend you've changed your mind, and you'd really rather look at the Cool Links page.
4. Click the Back button in the toolbar. This will take you immediately back to the Microsoft home page. Don't click Cool Links, though.

   Now, let's pretend that, after all, you *did* want to look at the Visit Microsoft page:
5. Click the Forward button in the toolbar. You will, once again, see the Visit Microsoft page.

That's all there is to it.

USING THE STOP BUTTON

The Stop button is the fifth button on your toolbar. Use the Stop button anytime you're in the middle of transferring a page, and you decide that you don't want to see it anymore. At that point, you can either exit the program, load in a different page, or go back to the previous page.

> TIP **Getting Graphic-Heavy Files** You can save time when retrieving documents with a lot of graphics and pictures. Open the View menu and select the Options command. You will see the Options dialog box. Clear the check from the box labeled *Show Pictures*.

Sometimes, pages will take a very long time to download. If you're trying to view a page at a very busy site, it can take several minutes to load a page. Oftentimes, you won't feel like waiting that long. Use the Stop button to stop the transfer, and then load a different page or go back to the previous page.

USING THE REFRESH BUTTON

The Refresh button is the sixth button on your toolbar. Use this button anytime you want to refresh the information on your screen. A common example would be the need to update a Web page that contains a weather map.

In this lesson, you learned how to get to your first Web page and how to use hypertext. You also learned how to use the basic toolbar buttons.

In the next lesson, you'll learn about the other buttons on the toolbar and the functions they perform. In the process, you'll learn how to surf the Net more productively.

LESSON 4

SURFING THE NET LIKE A PRO

In this lesson, you'll learn about other buttons on the toolbar and the functions they perform. You'll also learn more about surfing the Net more productively.

USING THE OTHER TOOLBAR BUTTONS

If you're not sure what I mean by "other buttons," jump back to the end of Lesson 3 where I discussed the first six buttons.

The remaining seven buttons don't really help you surf the Net, they just help you to configure Internet Explorer for your own tastes.

First, here is a list of these seven additional buttons, and a brief description of each:

BUTTON	FUNCTION
	Open Favorites
	Add to Favorites
	Use Larger Font
	Use Smaller Font

continues

continued

BUTTON	FUNCTION
	Cut
	Copy
	Paste

Again, to make things as easy as possible, I'll give a brief description of each button.

USING THE OPEN FAVORITES BUTTON

As you might expect, the Open Favorites button will cause Internet Explorer to open the Favorites folder in the main window.

For more information on how to use the Favorites folder, see Lesson 7. For information on how to organize and edit your Favorites folder, see Lesson 8.

USING THE ADD TO FAVORITES BUTTON

Use the Add to Favorites button anytime you run across a page you might want to view again. This will automatically add the current document URL to your Favorites folder.

For more information on how to use the Favorites folder, see Lesson 7. For information on how to organize and edit your Favorites folder, see Lesson 8.

Using the Use Larger and Use Smaller Font Buttons

To increase the size of the font Internet Explorer uses to display Web pages, click the Use Larger Font button. To decrease the size of the font, click the Use Smaller Font button.

Unfortunately, Internet Explorer does not allow you to change the font itself. Furthermore, you only have access to five sizes:

- Largest
- Large
- Medium
- Small
- Smallest

The actual size of these fonts will depend upon the resolution of your display adapter. To choose a specific size, open the View menu and choose the Fonts command. You will see a small submenu to the right of the View menu. Choose the size you'd like to use from this menu.

Using the Cut, Copy, and Paste Buttons

The Copy button allows you to highlight the text of a Web page and copy it to the Windows clipboard. From there, you can paste the information into another application.

The Cut and Paste buttons allow you to enter URLs into the Address Bar without having to type them out; you can also use the information in the Address Bar in another application. These buttons work just like the Cut, Copy, and Paste buttons in any

Windows program. Use them to cut, copy, and paste the URL in the Address Bar, or to copy text from a Web document. See Lesson 16 for more information on sharing information with other applications.

USING IMAGE MAPS

Another big step in the development of Web technology is the image map or image-sensitive map. These are standard inline graphics, but with an extra twist: if you click on an inline graphic, the Web browser transmits the coordinates of the mouse cursor relative to the upper-left-hand corner of the image.

This technology has a profound and exciting use. Instead of putting large, boring-looking bulleted lists all over the place, the Web page author can create a graphic that contains small icons for the place that you, the user, might want to visit. This makes it especially easy for novice, nontechnical users. If you're still confused, read on. I'll give you an example:

1. Open the File menu and select the Open URL command. You'll see the Open URL dialog box.
2. Type **http://www.home.msn.com** in the space provided and press Enter. Internet Explorer will begin to download the Microsoft home page. After it's complete (the logo in the top right-hand corner will stop "flying"), you will see the Web page shown in Figure 4.1.

FIGURE 4.1 The Microsoft home page.

3. Click on the word Explore in the image map. This will bring up the Explore the Internet page. You'll notice that this page also contains an image map at the top.

4. Click on the Reference Shelf image map. You'll see several good links to reference resources.

Remember: you can use the Back and Forward buttons on the toolbar if you want to visit more than one link from a specific page.

As you can see, this concept is just as easy to understand as traditional hypertext. If what I've been seeing is any indication, you'll be seeing a lot more of these image maps in the future. I guess people think they're cool. And they are.

Using Forms

Fill-out forms (usually called simply forms) allow a user to communicate with the Web server in more advanced ways. So far, we've been able to tell the server (in many different ways) which documents or pages we'd like to see. But, we've not been able to tell it, for example, who we are, what our favorite color is, or what kind of pizza we like.

HTML authors soon discovered a need to implement such capability into the World Wide Web. Thus, the age of forms was born.

Since forms can be difficult to explain, it is best to learn by example in this case. To see how forms work:

1. Open the File menu and select the Open command. You should see the Open Internet Address dialog box.
2. Type **http://www.pizzahut.com** in the space provided and press Enter. You should see the Pizza Hut home page, as shown in Figure 4.2. This page has three form fields in it. One for your name, one for your street address, and one for your home number. The Pizza Hut server uses this information to determine which Pizza Hut should cook your pizza and deliver it to you.
3. Fill out the form, then click the Continue button. This sends all the information to the Pizza Hut server, which determines the Pizza Hut location nearest you. If your area is not supported (very likely at this point) you'll see a page telling you just that. That page has a Demo button at the bottom. Click the Demo button to continue the example. Keep in mind, that this will not actually work if you've selected the Demo. Instead, you'll see a sample page that tells you where your order might have gone if you had really ordered a pizza.

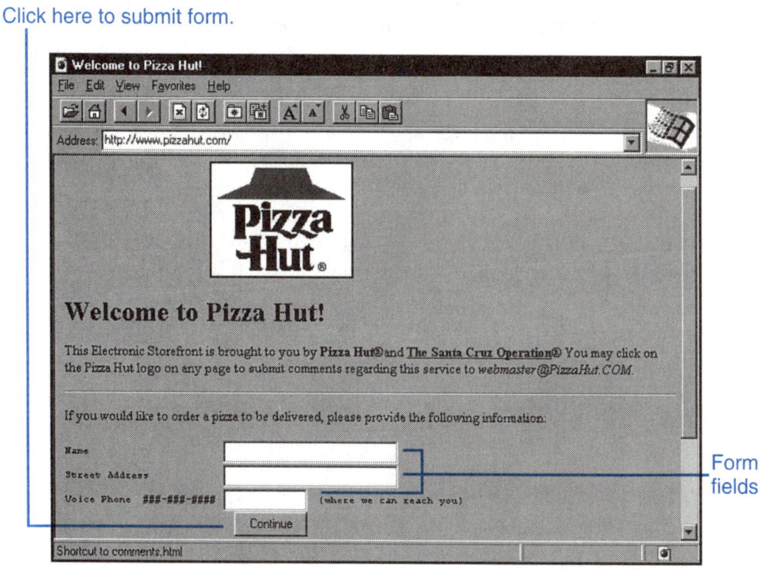

FIGURE 4.2 The Pizza Hut home page.

> **Be Careful With Forms!** It is best not to actually submit this form (since you might actually order a pizza you don't wish to pay for). This form, like many others on the Web, is used for commercial purposes. Since Internet Explorer doesn't support any security standards, you should not submit any personal information such as credit card numbers. I've used the Pizza Hut demo many times, and to my knowledge, Pizza Hut has not used my address for any commercial gain. See Lesson 17 for more information on shopping over the Internet.

4. Note that in some cases, you can choose from a dropdown list, in others, you can use check boxes, and in still other cases, you can actually type the information.

Forms are becoming vastly popular on the Internet. Some sites won't let you look at the pages until you've filled out some type of form, usually with your name and address. This way, they can use this information in an advertising campaign. Remember: somebody has to pay for all these computers, so companies are looking for ways for this to be profitable.

In this lesson, you learned about the other buttons on the toolbar and how to surf the Net more productively.

In the next lesson, you'll learn about the more advanced features of Web browsing. You'll also see some examples of the more complex Web resources.

NAVIGATING THE INTERNET

LESSON 5

In this lesson, you'll learn about the more advanced features of Web browsing. You'll also see some examples of the more complex Web resources.

UNDERSTANDING WORLD WIDE WEB TECHNOLOGY

The major Web browser companies (NCSA, Netscape, Spyglass, NaviSoft, and others) have contributed various technologies and features to Web browsing over the past year or two. These include:

- Different colors for links to pages you've already seen. These allow you to keep track of the places you've been, and make it much easier to explore the World Wide Web without revisiting places you've already seen, saving you tons of time.
- Image maps. We discussed image maps a bit in Lesson 4. These maps give a graphic alternative to traditional text-based hypertext. The process is simple: the Web browser transmits the mouse pointer coordinates relative to the top left-hand corner of the image. Since the server knows what the image looks like, it knows what you clicked on.
- Document and image cache. A cache is a temporary storage area. For our purposes, using the World Wide Web, your Web browser will retrieve each page and each graphic, and then keep them on your hard disk. This way, if you ever want to visit the same page again, or view the same graphic, the browser can reload the data from your hard disk. This is *much* faster than loading the

information from the Internet again; especially if you use the Internet over a modem. I'll explain it a bit more later in this lesson.

- Multiprotocol capability. Every Web browser has the capability to view HTML documents from Web servers. But newer browsers will also give you access to files, gopher menus, newsgroups, and more. Visit Lessons 13 and 14 for more information on how to access FTP file servers and gopher menu servers.
- Graphics capture. This feature gives the user the ability to save graphics images quickly and easily from the Web browser window. See Lesson 15 for more information on how to capture graphics with Internet Explorer.
- OLE support. OLE, or Object Linking and Embedding, gives you the ability to create shortcuts (or icons) to Web pages and paste them into other documents.
- Special links to Windows 95 features. Since Internet Explorer was written by Microsoft to work specifically under Windows 95, you get one-click access to many of Windows 95 features, like automatically using images you find in a Web page as your background wallpaper.

USING VISITED LINK COLORS

You may have noticed before, as you followed previous examples in this book, that, by default, links to pages you've already seen appear in purple instead of blue. This feature, along with the Go Back and Go Forward buttons, gives you, the user, the ability to quickly browse through all of the pages at a given site without retracing your steps and viewing information you've already seen.

Let's try a quick example to demonstrate this point:

1. Open the File menu and select the Open URL command. You will see the Open URL dialog box.
2. Type **http://www.einet.net** and press Enter. After a few moments, you will see the EINet Galaxy home page, as shown in Figure 5.1. Notice that this page is filled with hypertext links to hundreds of different topics and subtopics.

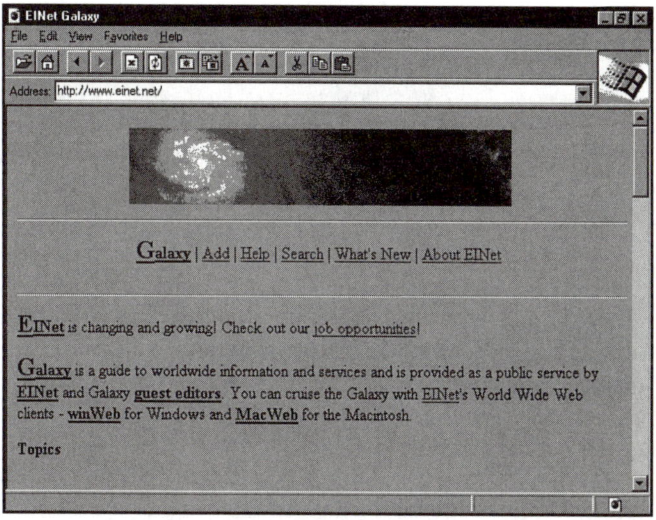

FIGURE 5.1 The EINet Galaxy home page.

3. To continue the example, click on the first topic. After the page is completed, click the Go Back button in the toolbar. You will see the EINet Galaxy home page again, but this time, the topic you've just clicked will appear in purple instead of blue. This indicates that you've already seen this page.

USING IMAGE MAPS

In order for a graphic to be considered an image map, it must instruct the Web browser to transmit the mouse coordinates relative to the top left-hand corner of the graphic. At that point, the server can determine the area you mean by the coordinates transmitted by the Web browser.

> **Image Map or Hyperlink?** First, it is important to understand that not all images are image maps. In some cases, the Web page author may create a hyperlink to a page using a normal graphic. If you were to click on that graphic, your Web browser would retrieve the document to which the graphic was linked. In this case, it would not matter where you clicked inside the graphic, just that you clicked the graphic. This is still considered a hyperlink, but not an image map.

Now, in order for this to work (luckily you won't need to do this yourself), the Web page author must program one or more areas of the graphic to link to one or more Web documents. Basically the process goes like this:

1. Specify a center point (usually in the center of the item the user would click).
2. Specify a shape (this could be a square, rectangle, circle, oval, etc.).
3. Specify a size.

With this information, the server software can "guess" which item you meant. For this reason, when using an image map, it is best to click as close to the center of an object, word, or icon as possible.

Sometimes, though, if you don't click close enough, or if you click on something that has no link associated with it, you'll simply see your screen flash, and then nothing else will happen. You won't get any error message. If this happens, take a closer look at the image to figure out what might be wrong.

USING A DOCUMENT AND IMAGE CACHE

For the most part, a document and image cache is a good thing. If you visit a page that contains a large number of graphics, for example, the next time you visit that page, you won't have to wait for all those graphics to come in again. The Web browser stores them on your hard disk for immediate access.

However, a document cache can, in fact, be a problem at times. If you're trying to view a document that frequently changes, such as a real-time weather map of your area, you'll get the same image you saw last time. This means the information won't be up to date, and therefore, won't be accurate. Also, the cache can begin to take up a lot of hard disk space. See Lesson 21 for information about configuring and maintaining a document cache.

In most cases, the best way to get a current Web page is to use the Refresh button on the toolbar.

If you don't wish to use the document cache it is possible to turn it off. See Lesson 21 for information on how to configure the document cache and other advanced features of Internet Explorer.

USING MULTIPROTOCOL CAPABILITY

If you've read Lesson 1, you'll remember our discussion of the URL as a Uniform Resource Locator. The URL can locate more than just Web pages. It can also locate gopher menus, file archives, and other useful resources on the Internet. We use the term "Uniform" because no matter what the type of resource, the format stays the same.

Internet Explorer has multiprotocol capabilities for three different Internet protocols:

- HTTP: The HyperText Transfer Protocol. This protocol is used for World Wide Web pages.
- gopher: This protocol is used to navigate gopher menus, a first generation hypertext menu browsing system. See Lesson 13 for more information on how to use gopher with Internet Explorer.
- FTP: File Transfer Protocol. This protocol is used to transfer binary files and images from a remote computer to your computer. See Lesson 14 for more information on how use FTP with Internet Explorer.
- mailto: This isn't really a protocol, but it tells Internet Explorer to use e-mail to send a message to another user on the Internet.

Each remote computer can detect which protocol your Web browser is trying to use. So, this makes the whole process of trying to access different types of information extremely easy for the user.

The University of Missouri (the "Show Me State") has a Web server, a gopher server, and an FTP server. I can access each of these independently of the other using one piece of software. Here's how:

Lesson 1 states that the first part of the URL specifies the protocol used to transfer the data. The software figures the rest out all by itself.

To access the World Wide Web server, type:

http://showme.missouri.edu

To access the gopher server, type:

gopher://showme.missouri.edu

To access the FTP server, type:

ftp://showme.missouri.edu

> **Disclaimer** Keep in mind, though, that not every site will have all three types of servers, so the above example does not apply in all cases. Also, some sites will have slightly different domain names for each server. For example:
>
> http://**www**.missouri.edu
>
> gopher://**gopher**.missouri.edu
>
> ftp://**ftp**.missouri.edu

Feel free to try the above example, though. Refer to Lessons 13 and 14 for a thorough explanation of gopher and FTP, and for more examples on how to use each.

In this lesson, you learned how to use the advanced Web browsing features of Internet Explorer, and you also saw some examples of the more complex Internet resources.

In the next lesson, you'll learn how to use the History folder to keep track of the documents you've already seen and how to use the History folder to share interesting documents with friends and coworkers.

LESSON 6

USING THE HISTORY FOLDER

In this lesson, you'll learn how to use the History folder to keep track of the documents you've already seen. You'll also learn how to use the History folder to share interesting documents with friends and co-workers.

VIEWING THE HISTORY FOLDER

Using the History folder is a handy method for keeping track of all the documents you've visited in the past. This folder is where Internet Explorer stores the URLs for each of these documents. You can access this History folder, change it, or use it to reload documents you've seen in the past.

To view the History folder:

1. Open the File menu and notice the numbered list of titles at the bottom, similar to that shown in Figure 6.1 (your entries may be different).

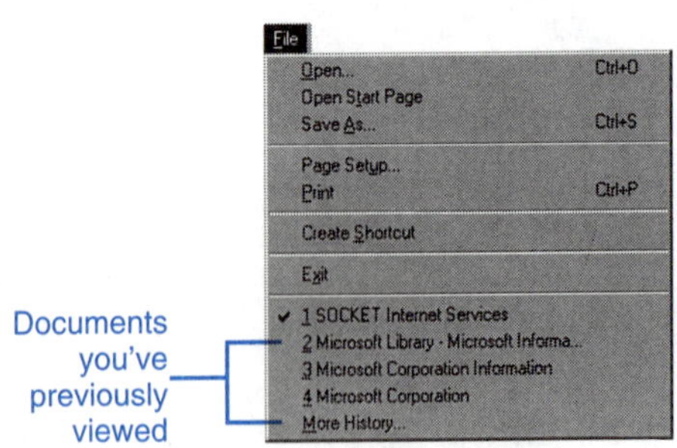

FIGURE 6.1 A sample History folder.

2. Click the title of the document you'd like to review.

This list of Web pages can be thought of as an "abbreviated history." To view a complete list of documents you've seen in the past:

1. Open the File menu and select the More History command at the bottom. Although the individual entries may be different, you will see a window similar to that shown in Figure 6.2.

Double-click a title to load the document in Internet Explorer.

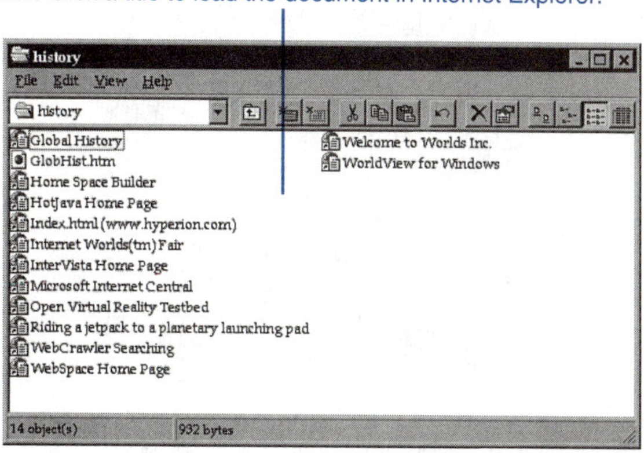

FIGURE 6.2 A complete list of documents in a History folder.

2. Double-click the title of a document to view it with Internet Explorer.

EDITING THE HISTORY FOLDER

As I mentioned in the previous section, the History folder is actually a list of small files that contain the URL of a Web page. These files exist in a directory on your hard drive. Lesson 21 tells you how to change the directory Internet Explorer uses to store your History folder.

As you might imagine, after a time, this History folder can become quite large. By default, Internet Explorer will store 300 document URLs in this directory. You can change this number, though. To change the number of entries Internet Explorer will store in the History folder:

1. Open the View menu and select the Options command. You'll see the Options dialog box, as shown in Figure 6.3.

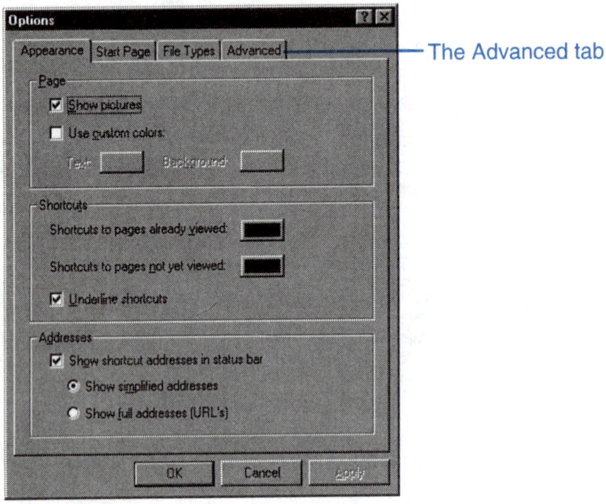

FIGURE 6.3 The Internet Explorer Options dialog box.

2. Click the Advanced tab at the top of the dialog box. The dialog will now resemble Figure 6.4.
3. Use the spin control to increase or decrease the number of documents stored in the History folder. You can also type a number in the edit field.

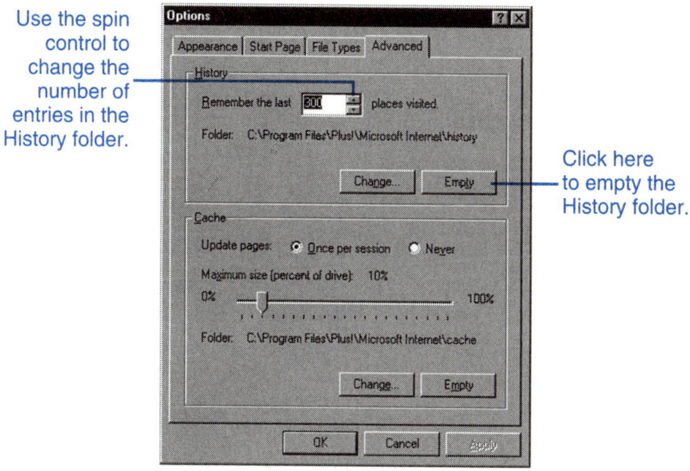

FIGURE 6.4 The Advanced options of Internet Explorer.

> **Spin Control** Next to numeric values, you will sometimes see a small up arrow and down arrow. These arrows increase or decrease the value in the field, similar to the "spinning" of the odometer in your car.

> **3,000 Is the Limit!** Do not use a number larger than 3,000. Internet Explorer will not display an error message telling you the number is too large, but it will not make the change.

4. Click OK to save your changes. You should be back at the main Internet Explorer window.

Oftentimes, you'll run across a document that you don't want kept in your History folder. Since the History folder is actually a directory of small files, you can perform any tasks with a History entry that you can with a file. To illustrate this:

1. Open the File menu and select the More History command at the bottom. You should see a window similar to that shown earlier in Figure 6.2. It will most likely look slightly different, though.
2. Click once on any entry in the History list. It should then be highlighted.
3. Right-click on the entry to bring up the menu shown in Figure 6.5.

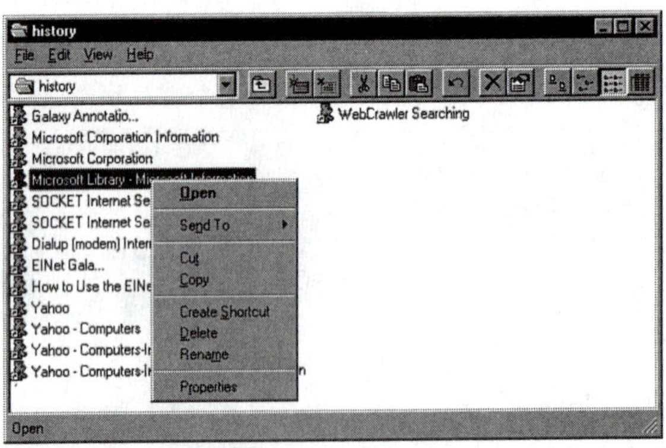

FIGURE 6.5 Use the right mouse button to get this menu.

As you can see from this menu, you can perform the following tasks (listed in the order they appear on the menu) on any entry in your History folder:

- Open This command performs the same function as double-clicking on the entry. Selecting the Open command will cause Internet Explorer to display this document in its window.

- Send To   Usually, this command will contain subcommands like 3 1/2 Floppy or Mail Recipient. Using the 3 1/2 Floppy subcommand allows you to save an URL to a floppy disk which you can give to a friend.

> **Mail Recipient**   If you've installed Microsoft Exchange on your computer, you will see this in your Send To menu. This command will automatically attach the currently highlighted file to a mail message which you can send via e-mail.

- Cut   This command is used to remove the URL from the History folder and place it elsewhere.
- Copy   This command is used to copy the URL from the History folder and place the copy in another location.
- Create Shortcut   This command will create a shortcut icon (an icon that points to the Web page) on your Desktop.
- Delete   This command will remove the item permanently from the History folder and place it in your Recycle Bin.
- Rename   This command will allow you to give the entry a different name. This is especially handy when the Web page in the list has no title, but only an URL.
- Properties   This command will display technical information about the URL file.

These commands will be explained in more detail in Lesson 16, which deals with sharing information with other applications and other users.

DELETING THE HISTORY FOLDER

If you've filled the History folder with more garbage than good information, you can empty it altogether and start over. To empty the History folder:

1. Open the View menu and select the Options command. You should see the Options dialog box, as shown earlier in Figure 6.3.
2. Click the Advanced tab at the top of the dialog box. The dialog should now resemble Figure 6.4 seen earlier.
3. Click the Empty button. Internet Explorer will ask if you're sure you want to empty the History folder.
4. Click Yes to empty the History folder.

In this lesson, you learned how to use the History List to keep track of the documents you've already seen and to share interesting documents with friends and coworkers.

In the next lesson, you'll learn how to use your Favorites folder to keep track of your favorite Web pages.

LESSON 7

Using Your Favorites Folder

In this lesson, you'll learn how to use the Favorites folder to keep track of your favorite Web pages. You'll also learn how to organize your Favorites folder to make reviewing documents simple and easy.

Adding a Web Page to Your Favorites Folder

To add a Web page to your Favorites folder:

(If you already see the document you wish to add, skip to step 3. Otherwise...)

1. Open the File menu and select the Open command. You will see the Open Internet Address dialog box.
2. Type the URL of the document you wish to see and press Enter. After a few moments, you will see the document in the Internet Explorer window.
3. Open the Favorites menu and select the Add To Favorites command. You will see the Add To Favorites dialog box as shown in Figure 7.1.
4. In the edit field labeled Name, you'll see a default name for the document. If you wish to change this, type a new name for the Web page.

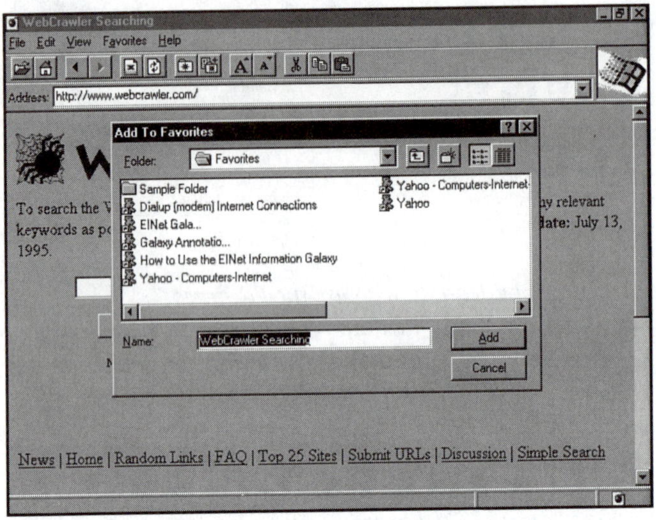

FIGURE 7.1 The Add To Favorites dialog box.

5. To add the entry, click Add. The Add To Favorites dialog box will disappear, and you'll be returned to the Internet Explorer window.

VIEWING YOUR FAVORITES

Having a list of Favorites is only a good thing if you retrieve that list and use it to reload a document into the Internet Explorer window. Internet Explorer allows you to use two different methods to view documents you've stored in your Favorites folder.

The first method lists the document in the Favorites menu in the Internet Explorer menu bar. To view the documents:

1. Open the Favorites menu. You will see a list of your documents at the bottom of this menu. If you've arranged your documents into folders (I'll show you how to do that at the end of this lesson), you'll notice submenus off this menu. Figure 7.2 gives an example. If you haven't added any documents yet, this menu will be empty.

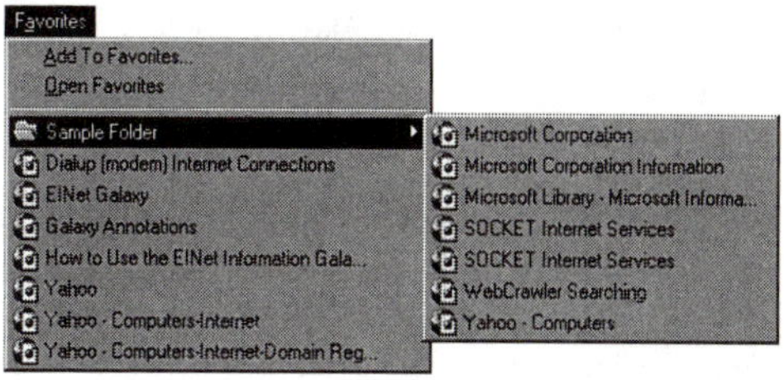

FIGURE 7.2 The Favorites menu.

2. To review a document in this menu, click the document you want to see. If the item exists in a submenu, highlight the submenu to view it, then move your mouse cursor to the document and click it.

The second method shows your Favorites as a folder on the hard disk. From this view, you can edit, delete, and move the entries. To view your Favorites folder:

1. Open the Favorites menu and select the Open Favorites command. You will see a window similar to the window shown in Figure 7.3. If you haven't added any documents yet, this folder will be empty.

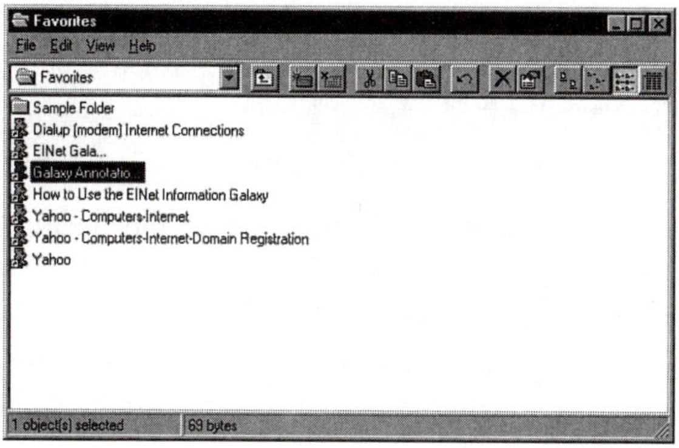

FIGURE 7.3 The Favorites folder.

2. To review a document in this list, double-click the document you want to see. The Favorites folder will disappear and, after a few moments, the document will appear in the Internet Explorer window.

Notice that most of the processes involved in reviewing Web documents involve only two steps. Internet Explorer goes out of its way to make Web browsing "as easy as 1, 2, 3." Well, make that "as easy as 1, 2!"

> TIP **Use Your Netscape Bookmarks!** If you've taken the time to create a large list of bookmarks with Netscape, you can use that list with Internet Explorer, too. Usually, your Netscape bookmark file is in your C:\NETSCAPE directory. The filename is BOOKMARK.HTM. Copy this file into your Favorites folder. Then, double-click it to view your bookmark as an HTML document.

Deleting a Web Page from Your Favorites Folder

Since the Web is a rapidly changing place, you may, at one point or another, create an entry in your Favorites folder that, after a while, no longer exists.

To delete a Web page from your Favorites folder:

1. Open the Favorites menu and select the Open Favorites command. You will see your Favorites folder (similar to that just shown in Figure 7.3).
2. Click once on the Web page you wish to delete, then right-click. You will see a small menu appear as shown in Figure 7.4.
3. Select the Delete command. You may be prompted to confirm the delete command. If so, click Yes to delete the entry.

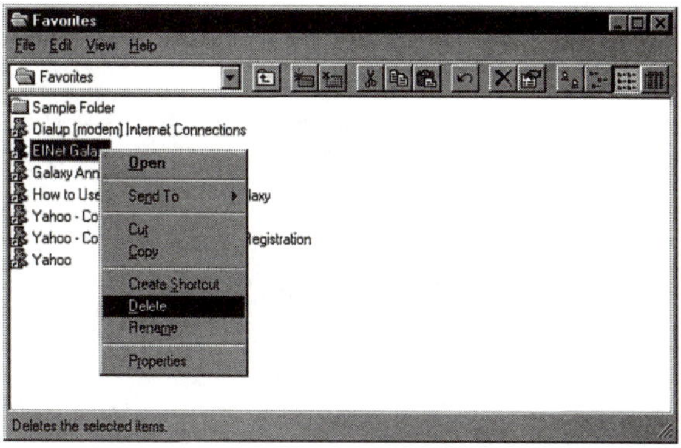

FIGURE 7.4 Select the Delete command to delete an entry.

If the page still exists, you don't have to delete the entry and start over; you can change the URL associated with it.

REORGANIZING YOUR FAVORITES FOLDER

Perhaps the finest feature of Internet Explorer is its ability to effectively organize large numbers of your favorite documents into an easy-to-use folder system. And, since each entry is really a file, you can cut, copy, paste, and move them just like you would any other file on your computer.

CHANGING THE PROPERTIES OF A FAVORITES FOLDER ENTRY

To change the URL for a document already in your Favorites folder:

1. Open the Favorites menu and select the Open Favorites command. You will see your Favorites folder (similar to that shown in Figure 7.3).
2. Click once on the Web page you wish to change, then right-click. A small menu will appear.

3. Select the Properties command. You will see the Properties dialog box.
4. Click the Internet Shortcut tab at the top of the dialog box. You will see the Yahoo Properties dialog box as shown in Figure 7.5.

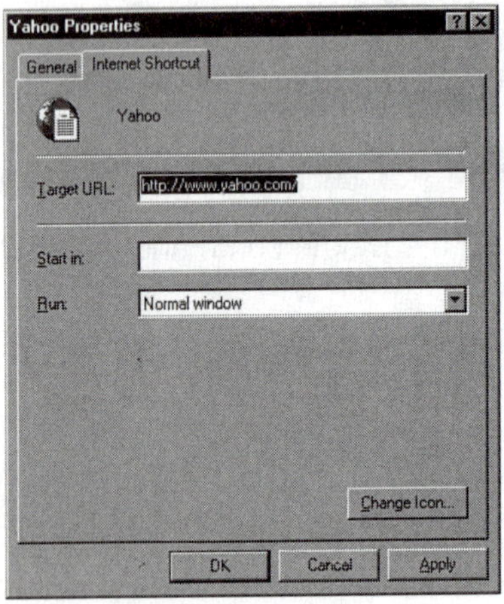

FIGURE 7.5 The Yahoo Properties dialog box.

5. In the field labeled Target URL, type the new URL for the document.
6. Click OK to save your changes.

ADDING ENTRIES FROM THE HISTORY FOLDER TO THE FAVORITES FOLDER

Another cool feature of Internet Explorer allows you to copy documents from your History folder to your Favorites folder. Remember, since both lists are actually directories on your hard drive, you don't even need to have Internet Explorer open to copy the entries (although it's easier that way). To copy an entry from your History folder to your Favorites folder:

1. Open the File menu and select the More History command. You will see your History folder.
2. Hold down the Ctrl key and click each document you wish to copy to your Favorites folder. Let go of the Ctrl key.
3. Right-click on one of the highlighted items. You will see a small menu appear.
4. Select the Copy command. The menu will disappear.
5. In the History folder window, open the File menu and select the Close command. You will be back at the Internet Explorer window.
6. Open the Favorites menu and select the Open Favorites command. You will see your Favorites folder.
7. Right-click inside the window of your Favorites folder. You will see another small menu.
8. Select the Paste command. You will see a Copying dialog box appear. After a few moments, the documents will appear in your Favorites folder.

In this lesson, you learned how to use the Favorites folder to keep track of your favorite Web pages. You also learned how to organize your Favorites folder to make reviewing documents simple and easy.

In the next lesson, you'll learn how to organize the documents in your Favorites folder to make them easier to use. You'll also learn how to change the properties of each document entry.

LESSON

8 Organizing Your Favorites Folder

In this lesson, you'll learn how to organize the documents in your Favorites folder to make them easier to use. You'll also learn how to change the properties of each document entry.

Renaming a Document in Your Favorites Folder

After I'd saved a large number of documents into my Favorites folder, I noticed that the names weren't always descriptive enough for me to remember what the page was all about. Although at the time, they made sense, after a few weeks, I didn't remember what they referred to anymore.

So, I renamed them to something more explanatory. You may run into the same situation after a few weeks of saving cool URLs to your Favorites folder. To rename a document:

1. Open the Favorites menu and select the Open Favorites command. You will see the Favorites folder.
2. Click the name of the document you wish to rename. It will be highlighted at this point.
3. Right-click the item again. You will see a small menu appear, as shown in Figure 8.1. This menu is the Context Functions menu.

> **Context Functions Menu** A small menu that appears when you right-click on an item, such as an icon or the desktop, that gives you a brief list of the most commonly accessed commands for that item. Windows 95 uses these menus quite frequently to give you quicker, easier access to the functions you need.

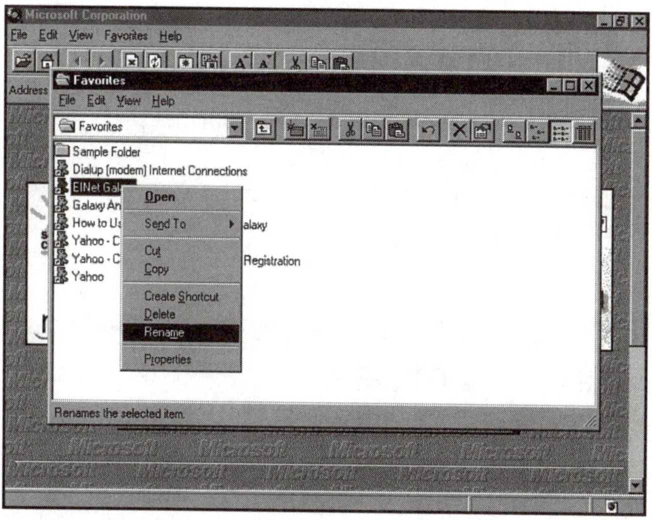

FIGURE 8.1 The context functions menu.

4. Select the Rename command from the menu. The name will appear as highlighted inside an edit field, and a cursor will be present at the end of the name, as shown in Figure 8.2.

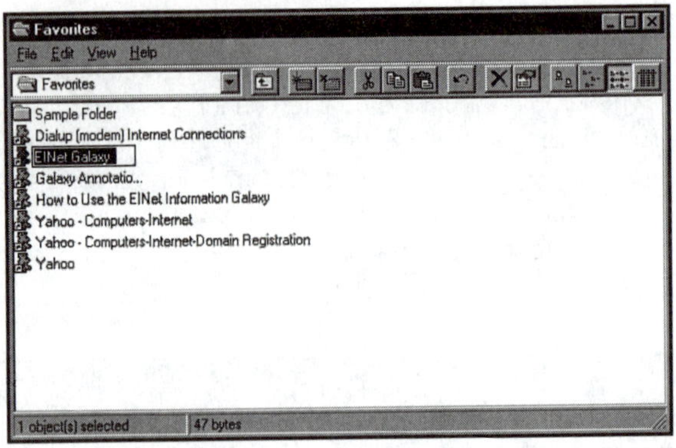

FIGURE 8.2 The document name as an edit field.

5. Type a new name for the document. Press Enter to save your changes.

CREATING SUBFOLDERS IN YOUR FAVORITES FOLDER

Perhaps the finest feature of Internet Explorer is its capability to effectively organize large numbers of your favorite documents into an easy-to-use menu system. And, since each entry is actually a file, you're probably already familiar with this procedure. I'll give you a review, though.

Most people create subfolders to organize the documents by subject. For example, my subfolders are named things like:

- Software Companies
- Hardware Companies
- Music
- Television
- Internet Service Providers

- Communications
- Cool Stuff

You can use names like this, or whatever works best for you. To create a subfolder in your Favorites folder:

1. Open the Favorites menu and select the Open Favorites command. You will see your Favorites folder.
2. Right-click in the window. You will see a small menu.
3. Select the New menu. You will see a submenu appear, as shown in Figure 8.3.

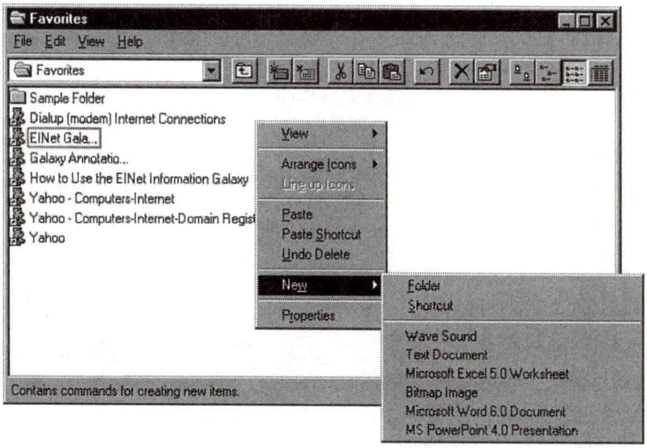

FIGURE 8.3 Create a new folder.

4. Select the Folder command from the submenu. A new folder will appear in the window. This folder's name will be highlighted.
5. Type a name for the folder. Your subfolder has been created.

At this point, you'll probably want to add some documents to this folder. I should point out that new documents will appear in the main folder. You'll have to move them if you want them to appear in a subfolder.

MOVING A DOCUMENT TO A SUBFOLDER

After you've created a subfolder, you'll likely want to move some of your existing documents into this folder. Or, you'll want to move future documents into it; remember, using the Add To Favorites command will add the document to the main Favorites folder only.

Luckily, this is an easy process. To move a document to a subfolder, simply drag it onto the subfolder.

You can move more than one document at a time, also:

1. Hold down the Ctrl key and click each document you wish to move.
2. After you've highlighted them all, let go of the Ctrl key.
3. Drag any one of the icons to the subfolder. This will move all the icons to the subfolder.

> TIP **Highlighting a Group of Files** If you want to highlight a group of files that are all in a row, click the first file, hold down the Shift key, then click the last file. The first file, the last file, and all of the files in between will be highlighted.

Although the methods just outlined are very easy, they only work when you wish to move documents to an immediate subfolder. If your Favorites folder structure is several levels deep, you'll need to follow a different procedure:

1. Hold down the Ctrl key and click each document you wish to move.
2. After you've highlighted them all, let go of the Ctrl key.
3. Right-click on one of the icons. You will see a small menu.

4. Select the Cut command. The icons you've highlighted will appear "grayed out."
5. Change to the subfolder where you'd like the icons to be.
6. Right-click in the window for that folder. You will see the small menu again.
7. Select the Paste command. You will see the Moving dialog box (if you only move a few, it might appear and disappear so fast you don't see it), and after a few moments, the entries will appear in this folder and be removed from the other folder.

CHANGING THE PROPERTIES OF A FAVORITES FOLDER ENTRY

Another frequent occurrence on the Internet: the document you are trying to view has "moved." This happens a lot when Web resources are bought out by corporations, or a student transfers. If you've created an entry in your Favorites folder for that page, you've got choices:

- Delete the entry and create a new one (Lesson 7 shows you how) or...
- Update the entry to reflect the new URL.

To change the URL for a document already in your Favorites folder:

1. Open the Favorites menu and select the Open Favorites command. You will see your Favorites folder.
2. Click once on the Web page you wish to change, then right-click. A small menu will appear.
3. Select the Properties command. You will see the Properties dialog box.

4. Click the Internet Shortcut tab at the top of the dialog box. You will see the EINet Galaxy Properties dialog box, as shown in Figure 8.4.

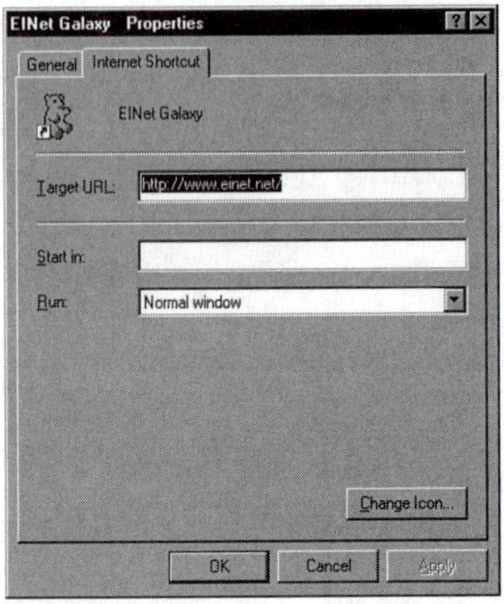

FIGURE 8.4 The EINet Galaxy Properties dialog box.

5. In the field labeled Target URL:, type in the new URL for the document.
6. Click OK to save your changes.

In this lesson, you learned how to organize the documents in your Favorites folder to make them easier to use. You also learned how to change the properties of each document entry.

In the next lesson, you'll learn how search engines work. You'll also learn how search engines keep track of the World Wide Web.

LESSON 9

Using Search Engines

In this lesson, you'll learn what a search engine is. You'll also learn how to use the EINet Galaxy to browse for information on the World Wide Web.

Understanding the Search Engine

Webster's New World Dictionary defines *engine* as "any machine that uses energy to develop mechanical power." Obviously, that's not we have here. However, Webster goes on to define *engineering* as the "the science concerned with putting scientific knowledge into practical uses..." With this in mind, let me propose this definition:

- search engine   A computer program that organizes a large amount of information into a database, and then performs ordered searches on that database based on keywords supplied by the user.

What does this mean for you? There are an estimated 50,000 Web servers on the planet today, and that number is growing fast. If you want to find a particular piece of information in that world, it's going to take a lot of time. With a search engine, you don't have to take that time. If you're looking for information about cars, you just type **cars**, and the computer does the rest, returning hundreds of links to Web pages about cars. If you're looking for Microsoft, just type **Microsoft** and you'll be on your way.

In my daily working life, I use three different search engines:

- The EINet Galaxy
- The WebCrawler
- Yahoo (I'm not sure where that name came from)

Of course, there are others, but these three are very popular, and I can always find what I need using one or more of these three. In this lesson, I'll give you an introduction to the EINet Galaxy, which is best suited for general searching. If you're looking for lots of information on a specific topic, see Lesson 10 on using WebCrawler. If you're looking for specific information, or a specific Web page, see Lesson 11 on using Yahoo.

Using the EINet Galaxy

EINet provides Internet access to private and corporate Internet users. As a service to its customers and the Internet community (although not a bad advertisement, either), EINet provides the EINet Galaxy pages.

This database of pages covers a wide range of topics presented to the user with a remarkably intuitive and easy-to-use interface.

Before I show you how to use it, let's bring it up. To get the EINet Galaxy pages:

1. Open the File menu and select the Open command. You should see the Open Internet Address dialog box.
2. Type **http://www.einet.net** and press Enter. After a few moments, you should see the EINet Galaxy home page, as shown in Figure 9.1.

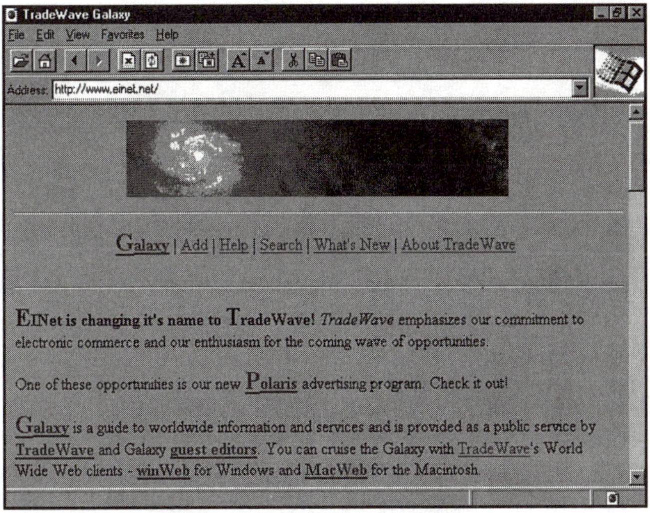

Figure 9.1 The EINet Galaxy home page.

Now that you're at the Galaxy home page, let's take a quick look around.

- The EINet menu bar contains quick access to the five main sections of the EINet Galaxy. I'll explain them later in this section.
- The Main section of the EINet home page consists of an organized list of topics. You can click on any topic (each word is a separate hypertext link) to view a sublist of additional, more specific topics.

Most of the links at the home page are to other pages on the Galaxy. If you browse deep enough, you'll eventually see documents from other places. Before you begin browsing here, though, let me explain the commands in the menu bar:

- Galaxy This link takes you to the main Galaxy page. If you're already there, this will have no obvious effect.

- Add This link takes you to a form that allows users to contribute information to the EINet Galaxy.
- Help This link takes you to the Help page (with a very cool graphic of the moon!). This page gives step-by-step instructions for accessing and searching for information at the EINet Galaxy and the rest of the World Wide Web.
- Search This link takes you to the search form. The user can type in a keyword, and the EINet search engine will look through the entire Galaxy for information on that topic. I'll explain how to use the search page in Lesson 10.
- What's New This link takes you to a large list of Galaxy pages that are less than seven days old. This a great place to go if you like to keep up with the latest stuff on the Web.
- About EINet This link takes you to an advertisement for EINet products and services.

To help you become more familiar with how the EINet Galaxy works, let's browse through a quick example:

1. If you're already at the main Galaxy page, skip to step 4. Otherwise...
2. Open the File menu and select the Open command. You will see the Open Internet Address dialog box.
3. Type **http://www.einet.net** and press Enter. After a few moments, you will see the main EINet Galaxy page.
4. In the first listing, entitled Arts and Humanities, select the Performing Arts hyperlink. After a few moments you will see the Performing Arts Galaxy page.
5. In the list of topics, select the Music hyperlink. After a few moments, you will see the Music page.

> **TIP** **No Need for http://** On most sites, you can type the address of the site without the http:// part. For example, you can type **www.einet.net** and press Enter. Internet Explorer will automatically assume you mean http:// and include it for you.

This page is filled with links to information about music as an academic pursuit. As you can see from the top of this page, if you were looking for information on music performance, instead, convenient links to the right place are provided. Features like this make the EINet Galaxy a breeze to use for beginners, and a great place to do a little information searching, even for the most advanced user.

I also use the EINet Galaxy if I'm not looking for anything in particular, but just browsing around. After all, the Internet can be a wonderful source of relaxation, too.

Using the EINet Galaxy Search Page

As I mentioned above, the EINet Galaxy has search capabilities, as well. This search engine helps you to locate information on the Galaxy itself, as well as the rest of the World Wide Web. To demonstrate, let's use the example of music. To search the EINet Galaxy for information about music:

1. If you're already at the EINet Galaxy home page, skip to step 4. Otherwise...
2. Open the File menu and select the Open command. You will see the Open Internet Address dialog box.
3. Type **http://www.einet.net** and press Enter. After a few moments, you will see the EINet Galaxy home page.

4. In the menu at the top of the page, select the Search link. After a few moments, you will see the Searching the Galaxy page as shown in Figure 9.2.

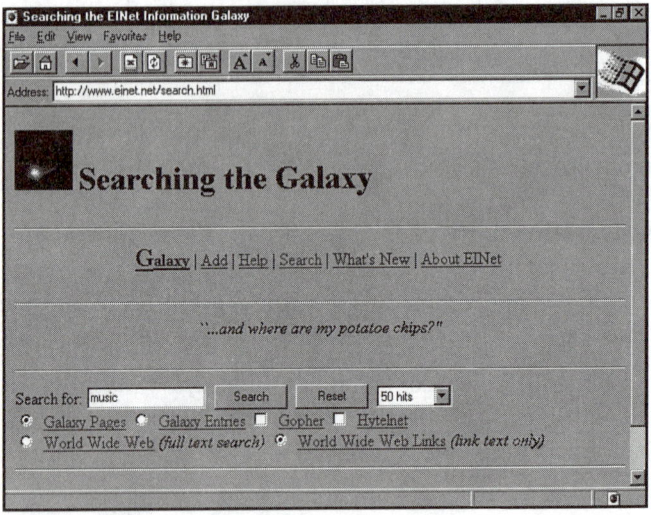

FIGURE 9.2 The ElNet Galaxy search page.

5. In the Search for: edit field, type **music** (or another topic, if you'd rather).

6. Use the radio buttons and check boxes below the edit field to specify the type of information resources you wish to view. *An explanation of each type follows this list.*

7. Click Search to start your search. You will see a list of hyperlinks similar to that shown in Figure 9.3.

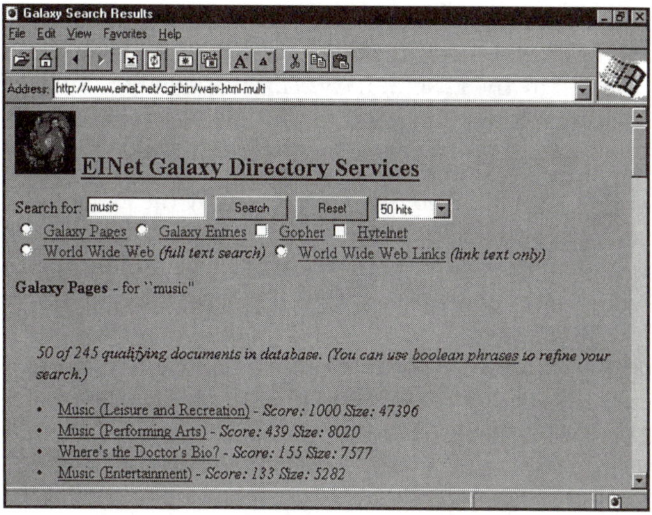

FIGURE 9.3 A sample search result window.

By default, an EINet search will return EINet Galaxy pages. Sometimes, you might want a different type of list. Here's a brief explanation of each type:

- **Galaxy Pages** This index contains only pages in the EINet Galaxy itself. Use this type to find collections of references related to your keyword.
- **Galaxy Entries** This index contains only the titles of pages in the EINet Galaxy. Use this type to find information on very specific information (such as "Microsoft").
- **Gopher** This index contains titles of gopher menus. To learn more about gopher, see Lesson 13.
- **Hytelnet** This index contains references to the hypertext telnet database.

- World Wide Web Text This index contains the full text of hundreds of thousands of World Wide Web pages referenced by the EINet Galaxy. This helps you to find very specific information resources not included in the Galaxy.
- World Wide Web Links This index contains all the links to World Wide Web pages referenced by the EINet Galaxy. Use this search to find very specific references. This search returns only World Wide Web pages that contain your keyword in the URL of the document.

If you find the above list overwhelming, don't worry. When you execute a search, don't select any particular resource type, and you'll get a comprehensive list of great information. Also, feel free to visit the Help page for more detailed information on how to increase the power of your EINet Galaxy searches.

OTHER SEARCH ENGINES

Although this lesson used the EINet Galaxy to demonstrate the search engine, you'll find many search engines available on the Internet. If you want to peruse them, just type in the URLs:

- World Wide Web Worm **http://www.cs.colorado.edu/home/mcbryan/WWWW.html**
- WebCrawler **http://www.webcrawler.com**
- Yahoo **http://www.yahoo.com**
- CUSI **http://web.nexor.co.uk/public/cusi/cusi.html**
- Lycos **http://www.lycos.com**

In this lesson, you learned what a search engine is. You also learned how to use the EINet Galaxy to browse for information on the World Wide Web.

In the next lesson, you'll learn how to use the WebCrawler to locate large amounts of information on broad topics.

Searching for Documents by Keyword

LESSON 10

In this lesson, you'll learn how to use WebCrawler to search for documents by keyword.

Understanding Keyword Searches

When you search for something with a keyword, the search engine looks for the keyword in a large list of documents. For example, if I type **fish** as a keyword, the search engine will look through every document and return to me a list of those documents that contain the word fish.

The same is true with multiple-word searches. WebCrawler, unlike some other search engines, uses an "implied and" between each keyword. A search for **race car driver** will return documents that contain the word *race,* the word *car,* and the word *driver*—though not necessarily together or in their original order.

Also, the WebCrawler strips certain words out of the document (like *the, and, be, or, not, to, web*) before it saves them. These words are in virtually every document on the Internet, so they're not really all that useful. However, this means that a search on **to be or not to be** is not possible.

WebCrawler is a powerful search engine because it gets its information from a software "robot" called a Crawler. The Crawler, pretending to be a user, continually cruises the Web for new Web pages, indexing new sites as it goes. Another type of robot is called a Worm. The World Wide Web Worm (**http://www.cs.colorado.edu/home/mcbryan/WWWW.html**) has the same capabilities as WebCrawler, but is accessed so frequently that it's very tough to connect with.

PERFORMING A SIMPLE SEARCH

As powerful as WebCrawler is, it's also a great search tool for beginners because of its simple and easy-to-use interface. To search the World Wide Web using the WebCrawler:

1. Open the File menu and select the Open command. You should see the Open Internet Address dialog box.
2. Type **http://www.webcrawler.com** and press Enter. After a few moments, you should see the WebCrawler search page, as shown in Figure 10.1. It might be a good idea to add this document to your Favorites folder. To find out how, see Lesson 7.

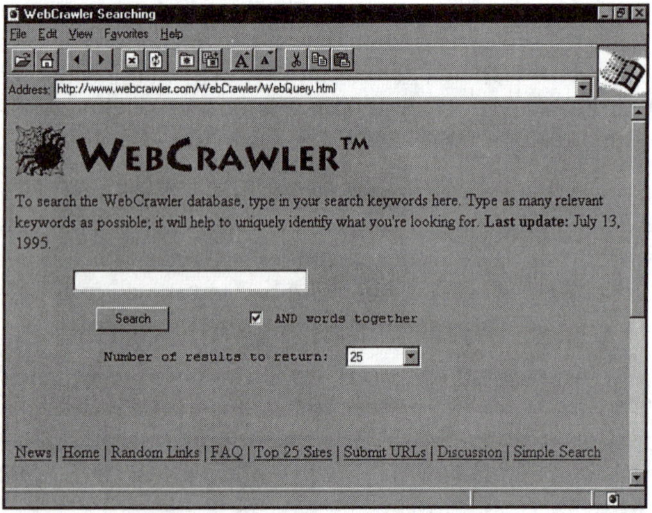

FIGURE 10.1 The WebCrawler search page.

3. Above the Search button, you'll see a blank edit field (it's not labeled at all). Type **music** (or another topic, if you'd rather) and click Search. After a few moments, you should see a results windows similar to that shown in Figure 10.2. Note that WebCrawler found about 10,000 documents.

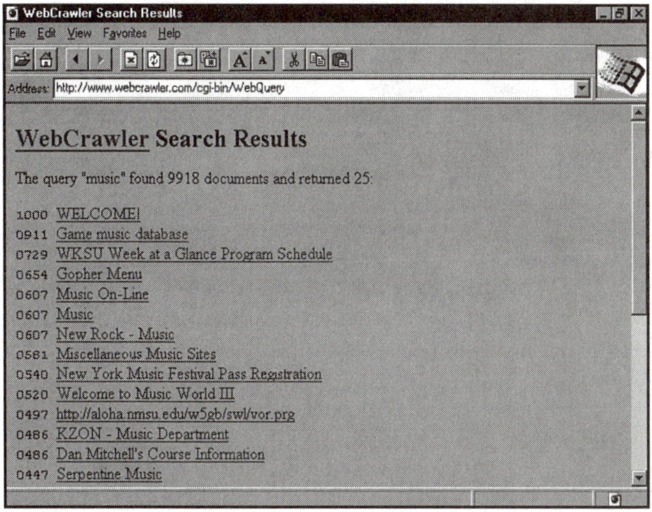

FIGURE 10.2 A sample search results window.

4. Each item in the search results list is a link to a document that relates to your search query. To view that document, click the link once.

> **What's This Error Message?** Every once in a while, WebCrawler will be busy; so busy that it cannot handle the load of another query. When this happens, you'll get an error message. If this happens, wait a few minutes, and then try again—or try another search engine.

You've probably noticed a number to the left of each link. That number ranks the link; the larger the number, the more relevant that particular page is to your query. WebCrawler follows three simple rules:

- The more frequent your keyword appears on a page, the more relevant it is. A page that contains your keyword

100 times is more relevant than a page that only contains the word once.

- A page that contains your keywords in the order you typed them and right next to one another is more relevant than a page that contains all the words, but scattered throughout the document.
- The most relevant page will always receive a rating of 1000. The other pages are numbered based on a rating relative to 1000. 1000 means that the document found is the most pertinent one, with lesser numbers used for less relevance.

The numbers are especially useful for many-word searches. But for most searches, I usually just start at the top of the list, and work my way down until I find something useful to my project.

PERFORMING ADVANCED SEARCHES

In most cases, you can get lots of information by searching on a single keyword. This is usually the best way to search with the WebCrawler. However, as in the case above, the WebCrawler will provide thousands of links related to your keyword. **Music**, for example, may be a bit too broad a topic for an effective search. We can, then, give the WebCrawler more specific information by simply providing more than one word. Only documents that contain all of the words we specify will be provided in the search results.

Let's try a more pointed query:

1. If you're already at the WebCrawler search page, skip to step 4. Otherwise...
2. Open the File menu and select the Open command. You should see the Open Internet Address dialog box.
3. Type **http://www.webcrawler.com** and press Enter. You should see the WebCrawler search page, as shown in Figure 10.1.

4. Above the Search button, you'll see a blank edit field (it's not labeled at all). Type **music baroque Bach** and click Search. After a few moments, you should see a results windows similar to that shown in Figure 10.3. This time, WebCrawler only found 23 documents.

5. Again, each item in the search results list is a link to a document that relates to your search query. To view that document, click the link once.

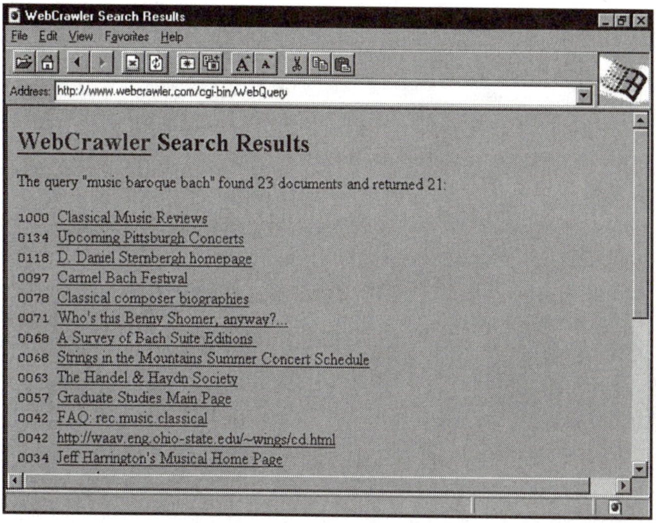

FIGURE 10.3 Another sample document list.

> TIP
>
> **Three to Five Is the Rule** As you can see, these documents are much more specific to the topic than when we searched on **music** alone. However, in some cases, you might be too specific. For example, **music baroque bach organ notation concert performance** is probably too specific. I recommend using three to five keywords in most cases. If you get too many documents, try to add another one. If you don't get enough, try to leave one out.

Also, if you'd like to see more than 25 documents returned to you, use the dropdown listbox to specify a larger number. 500 is the largest number allowed.

In this lesson, you learned how to use WebCrawler to search for documents by keyword.

In the next lesson, you'll learn how to use Yahoo to search for documents on the World Wide Web by category.

Searching for Documents by Category

LESSON 11

In this lesson, you'll learn how to use Yahoo to search for documents on the World Wide Web by category.

Understanding Category Searches

In the last lesson, I explained how to use keyword searches to search for information. Category searches work a bit differently, and can be easier to use, depending upon the task at hand. In most cases, a category search is good if you're not sure exactly what you're looking for.

On the other hand, I also use it a lot to find very specific information, like: "Where is AT&T's home page?" How are both of these possible? I'll demonstrate.

Using Yahoo

Yahoo, like the EINet Galaxy, has a menu of choices at the top of each page to facilitate the use of the system (see fig. 11.1). Here's a brief description of each link:

- New   This button takes you to a list of new entries in the Yahoo database.
- Cool   This button takes you to the Yahoo list of cool Web sites.
- Headlines   This button takes you to a list of top stories, both about the computing industry, and about other areas of interest as well.

- Popular This button takes you to a list of the most popular categories in the Yahoo database.
- Write Us This button takes you to a form you can use to submit comments to Yahoo administrators.
- Add URL This button takes you to a form you can use to add an URL or Web site that you find interesting, but doesn't exist in the Yahoo database, yet.
- Random This button will take you to a random place on the Internet. There's no telling what you'll see, so you may want to beware. Most of these links are not offensive, but some may be.
- Info This button takes you the Yahoo Information Center. This page will answer your questions about Yahoo and give you information about how it works and changes that may be taking place at Yahoo.

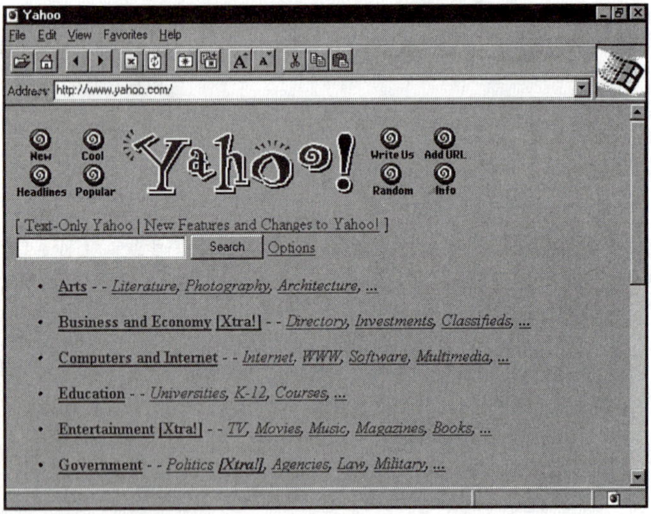

FIGURE 11.1 The Yahoo menu.

FINDING GENERAL INFORMATION

Since Yahoo is divided into categories, you can use the menu system to find huge lists of information on just about any topic. Here's a general example:

1. Open the File menu and select the Open command. You should see the Open Internet Address dialog box.
2. Type **http://www.yahoo.com** and press Enter. After a few moments you should see the Yahoo home page, as shown in Figure 11.2.

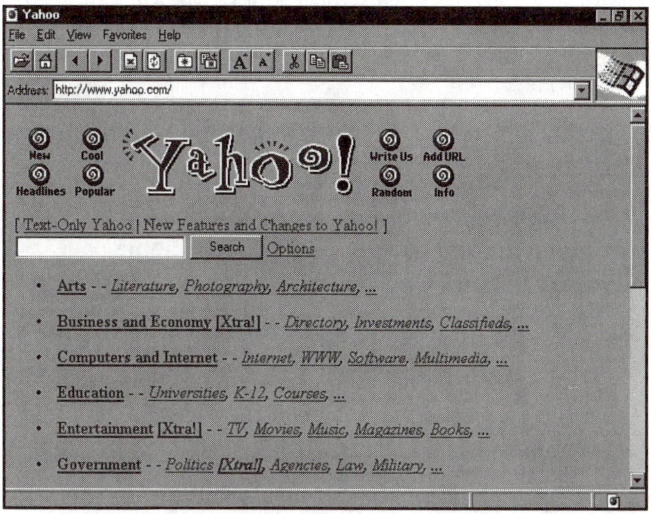

FIGURE 11.2 The Yahoo home page.

3. Assuming we still want to find information about music, click Entertainment. You should see a sublist of entertainment categories.
4. In this list, click Music. You may need to use the scroll bar to go down the page a bit. You should see a sublist of music categories.

From this list, you can find thousands of documents about music, either specific to a subject, or just generally about music. I usually use this method to browse about subjects that I find to be interesting, like music, computers, and the Internet.

FINDING SPECIFIC INFORMATION

You can also use Yahoo to be very specific, as well. As a matter of fact, I use Yahoo almost exclusively to find that one particular page that I know I've seen before, but I can't remember where it was. Let's say I want to find Macmillan Publishing. By searching the categories, I can find just what I'm looking for:

1. If you're already at the Yahoo home page, skip to step 4. Otherwise...
2. Open the File menu and select the Open command. You should see the Open Internet Address dialog box.
3. Type **http://www.yahoo.com** and press Enter. After a few moments you should see the Yahoo home page, as shown in Figure 11.2.
4. Since Macmillan is a business, click the Business link. You should see a list of business categories.
5. Click the Corporations link. You should see a list of types of corporations.
6. Since Macmillan is a book publisher, click the Books link. You should a long list of book publishers of all types.
7. If you use the scroll bar on the right side of your windows, you can traverse the list of book publisher. Alas, you've found Macmillan Publishing, and you can use that link to go straight to the Macmillan Publishing Bookstore home page.

Note that as an added bonus, I've found links to many other publishers as well.

Searching Yahoo for Information

As if Yahoo isn't already a very cool thing, you can also use a search engine on Yahoo. Since it's organized differently from the EINet Galaxy and the WebCrawler, your search result can be pleasingly on-target. Let's use the music example as well as the Macmillan Publishing example for this search.

1. First let's get to the search page. If you're already at the Yahoo page, click the Search command in the menu at the top of the page. Otherwise...
2. Open the File menu and select the Open command. You will see the Open Internet Address dialog box.
3. Type **http://www.yahoo.com/search.html** and press Enter. If you're at the Yahoo home page, you can also use the **Search** hyperlink. You will see the Yahoo search page as shown in Figure 11.3. You'll probably want to add this page to your Favorites folder. To find out how, see Lesson 7.

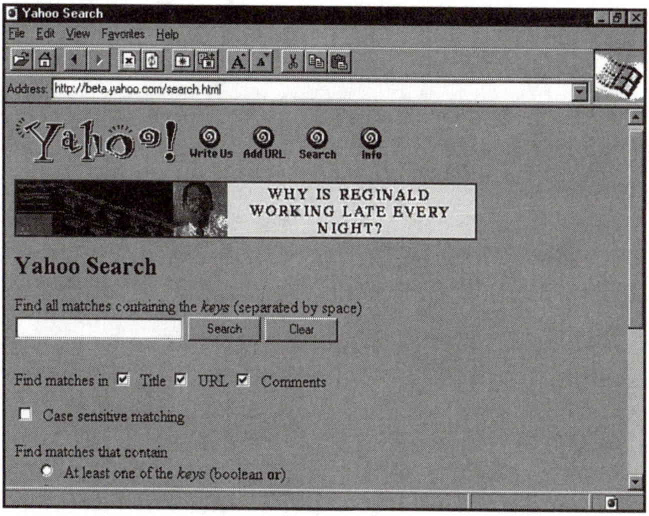

Figure 11.3 The Yahoo search page.

Now, let's perform the two searches and compare the results. First the general topic search on music:

1. In the edit field, type **music** and press Enter.
2. After a few moments, you should see a search results window. If a link looks interesting to you, click it.

As you can see, using a Yahoo search on a broad topic with Yahoo delivers sometimes undesirable results. You would have been better off to use the category structure (Entertainment/Music) from the Yahoo home page. Don't get me wrong, though; the results are still usable.

Let's try the Macmillan Publishing search, a more specific search:

1. Click the Search link in the menu at the top of the page to get back to the search page, as shown in Figure 11.3.
2. In the edit field, type **Macmillan Publishing** and press Enter.
3. After a few moments, Yahoo presents you with a list of the results which contain links to Macmillan's various Web pages.

With Yahoo, it is necessary to think out your search specifically. Here are my suggestions:

- If you're looking for a wide range of documents about a general subject, start at the home page and click through the category lists. You'll generally find a lot more good information. You might also try using the WebCrawler (explained in Lesson 10) and use keyword searches.
- If you're looking for a specific document or specific topic, use the Yahoo search feature. Also, since Yahoo is operated by America Online, commercial sites will pay money for a listing on Yahoo. Therefore, the search feature will return great information of a commercial nature, if that's what you're looking for.

CUSTOMIZING YOUR YAHOO SEARCH

As I mentioned earlier, you'll find a section of radio buttons and check boxes underneath the edit field, as shown in Figure 11.4.

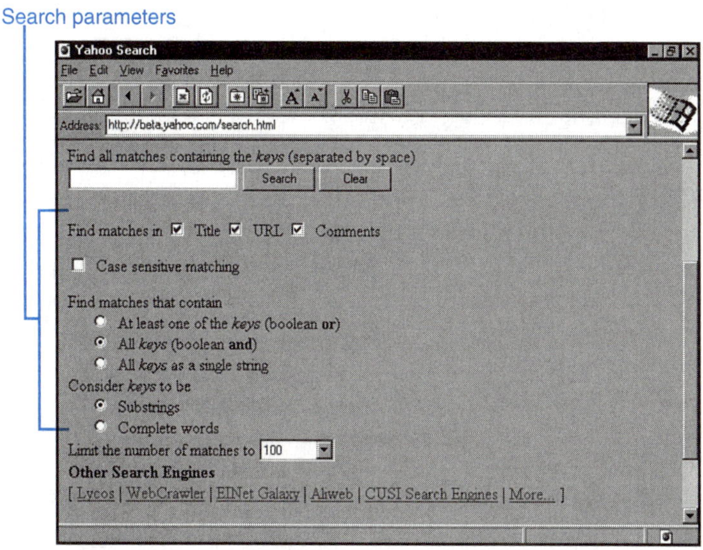

FIGURE 11.4 Yahoo search parameters.

The first item, labeled Find matches in tells the search engine where to look for the text you've typed in the edit field:

- Title This tells Yahoo to look in the HTML title of the document. This is the text that appears on your title bar when you view the document.
- URL This tells Yahoo to look in the URL, or Internet Address, of the documents for the text. This is handy if you want a search query like Intel to return a document whose URL is **http://www.intel.com** even if the word *Intel* isn't in the document at all.
- Comments This tells Yahoo to look in the comments for the search query. This is usually not very useful, but an option nonetheless.

Yahoo will always search the text of the document for your search query, but you can remove the checks from these boxes to prevent searching of these entities.

The second item, labeled Case sensitive matching, tells Yahoo whether to perform a case-sensitive search. If a search is not case sensitive, a search on datastorm will return any document containing datastorm, DataStorm, or DATASTORM. With a case-sensitive search, capitalization must match exactly.

The third item, labeled Find matches that contain, allows you to specify the function of your keywords. For example, if you wanted to search for baroque music, you would want to specify a Boolean and (meaning: I want to find all documents that contain the word Baroque *and* the word music). I could also specify a Boolean or and search for Baroque Classical Romantic Rococo. This would return a list of documents that contained the word Baroque *or* Classical *or* Romantic *or* Rococo, giving me a Web page about art music in general. Finally, I can specify that the list of keywords is a string. This is useful if want to find the Cool Site of the Day page. Those words are in a lot of documents, but only in a few are they actually in that order as a phrase. This helped me to find that site in seconds.

The fourth item, labeled Consider keys to be, tells Yahoo whether or not your keyword should be considered a substring or a complete word. What's the difference? Well, if you set this to Complete words, then Yahoo will only return documents that contain the word you typed. If you set this to substring, then Yahoo will return documents that contain that set of letters in that order. Confusing? Here's an example: a substring search on Web would return documents that contained words like *web, webber, weber, webbed,* etc. A complete word search would ignore *webber, weber,* and *webbed.*

In this lesson, you learned how to use Yahoo to search for documents on the World Wide Web by category.

In the next lesson, you'll learn how to find new and cool Web sites using several tools available on the World Wide Web.

SEARCHING FOR NEW AND COOL WEB SITES

LESSON 12

In this lesson, you'll learn how to find new and cool Web sites using several tools available on the World Wide Web.

USING COOL SITE OF THE DAY

When the World Wide Web first began to show worldwide popularity, many of the people who first begin using it wanted to find a way to see all the new sites as they came up. Well, of course, that quickly became impossible to do.

One of the instant hits of this battle, though, was a Web page called Cool Site of the Day. This page, and others like it, provide a single link to a cool site that they've found. This link is changed once a day.

To visit the Cool Site of the Day:

1. Open the File menu and select the Open command. The Open Internet Address dialog box will appear.
2. Type **http://www.infi.net/cool.html** and press Enter. After a few moments, you will see a document that resembles the one shown in Figure 12.1. Yours will look different, of course.

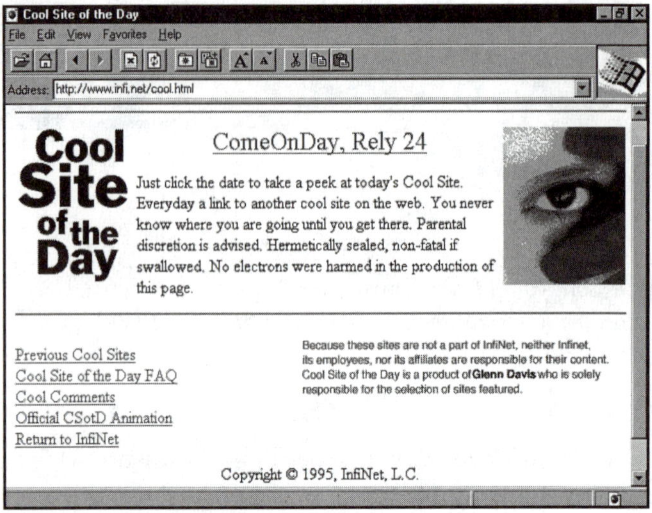

FIGURE 12.1 Cool Site of the Day.

3. Click the date at the top of the page to visit the Cool Site of the Day.

Notice that the date is usually written out with odd words that sound like the date. When I last looked at it, it read: **ComeOnDay, Rely 24**. This means Monday, July 24. Pretty cool, huh?

You can also view previous Cool Sites of the Day. Just follow the link that reads Previous Cool Sites.

NEW AND COOL SITES FROM NETSCAPE

Netscape Communications, the company that publishes the popular Netscape Navigator, offers two spectacular lists of links on their Web server: What's New and What's Cool. Each list contains lots of great sites, and Netscape keeps them fairly up to date.

To find the What's New list:

1. Browse to **http://home.mcom.com/escapes/whats_new.html**. You will see the What's New page, as shown in Figure 12.2.

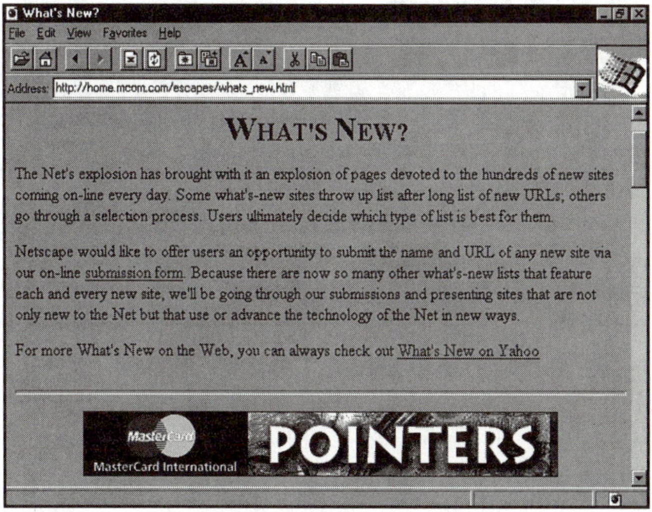

FIGURE 12.2 Netscape's What's New collection.

2. Use the scroll bar on the right-hand side of the window to browse through the list. Each item has a description. If one sounds interesting, click the link.

To find the What's Cool list:

1. Open the File menu and select the Open command. You should see the Open Internet Address dialog box.

2. Type **http://home.mcom.com/escapes/whats_cool.html** and press Enter. After a few moments, you should see the What's New page, as shown in Figure 12.3.

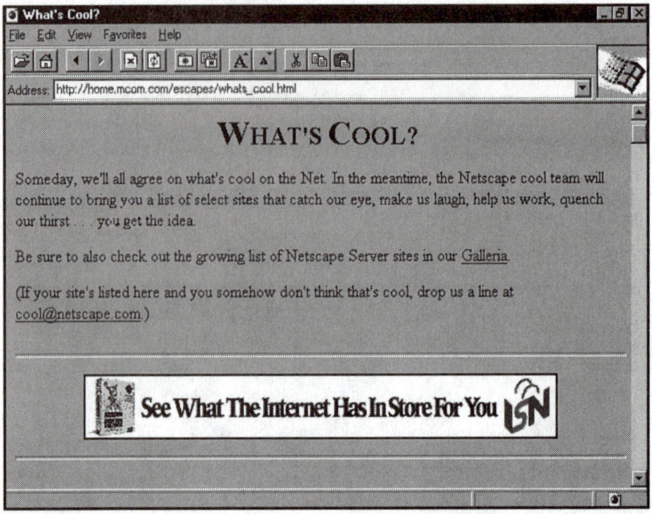

FIGURE 12.3 Netscape's What's Cool collection.

3. Use the scroll bar on the right-hand side of the window to browse through the list. Each item has a description. If one sounds interesting, click the link.

WHAT'S NEW AND COOL ON YAHOO

Yahoo, which we visited in Lesson 11, also keeps track of its new entries on a daily basis. As Yahoo adds between 100 and 800 sites a day, it's very difficult to keep track of them all.

1. Open the File menu and select the Open command. You should see the Open Internet Address dialog box.
2. Type **http://www.yahoo.com/new** and press Enter. After a few moments, you should see the What's New on Yahoo page, as shown in Figure 12.4.

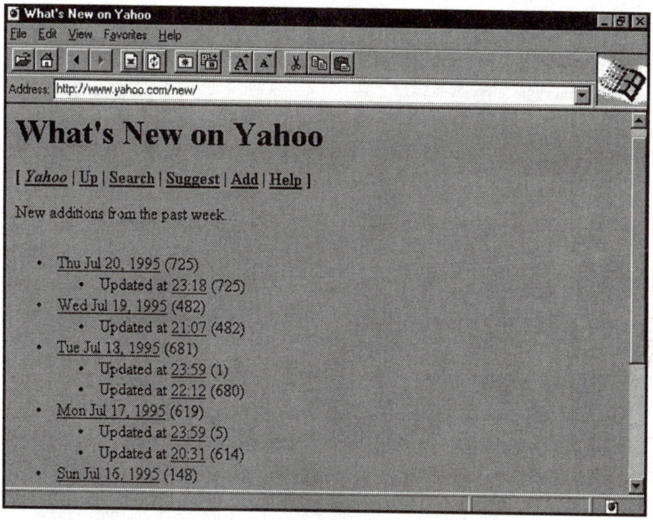

FIGURE 12.4 What's new on Yahoo.

3. Use the scroll bar on the right-hand side of the window to browse through the list. Each item has a description. If one sounds interesting, click the link.

Yahoo also maintains a collection of cool sites. You can find this list from the Yahoo home page by selecting Entertainment and then COOL Links. Or...

1. Open the File menu and select the Open command. You should see the Open Internet Address dialog box.
2. Type **http://www.yahoo.com/Entertainment/COOL_links** and press Enter. After a few moments, you should see the What's Cool on Yahoo page, as shown in Figure 12.5.

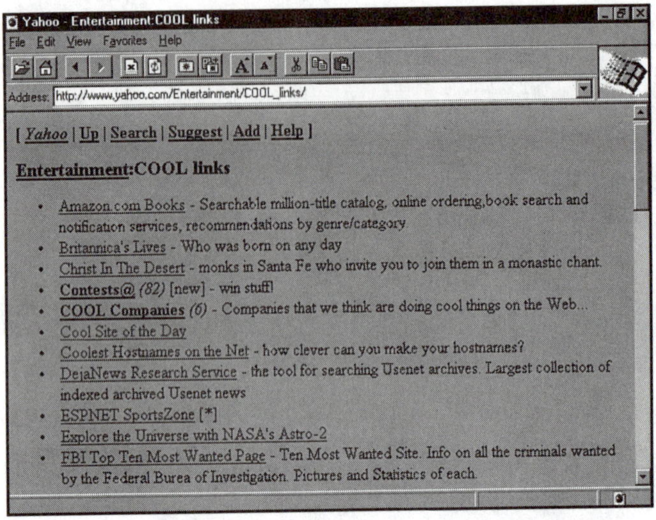

FIGURE 12.5 What's Cool on Yahoo.

3. Use the scroll bar on the right-hand side of the window to browse through the list. Each item has a description. If one sounds interesting, click the link.

WHAT'S NEW AT THE EINET GALAXY

The EINet Galaxy also maintains a list of new sites, as well. As with Yahoo, this list represents links that have recently been added to the category lists. At EINet, they keep track of all links added within the past seven days.

To access this list:

1. Open the File menu and select the Open command. You should see the Open Internet Address dialog box.
2. Type **http://www.einet.net/galaxy/new-links.html** and press Enter. After a few moments, you should see the Galaxy Pages Containing New Items page, as shown in Figure 12.6.

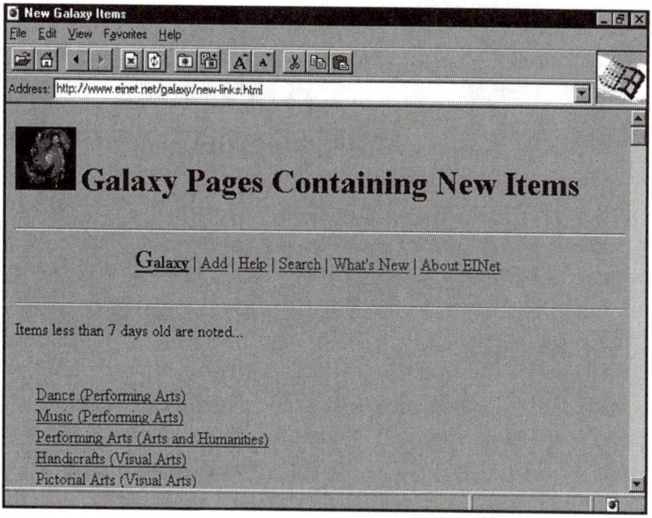

FIGURE 12.6 The Galaxy Pages Containing New Items page.

3. Use the scroll bar on the right-hand side of the window to browse through the list. If an item sounds interesting to you, click the link to view it.

As you can see, most of the pages listed here are Galaxy pages, not actual World Wide Web pages.

In this lesson, you learned how to find new and cool Web sites using several tools available on the World Wide Web.

In the next lesson, you'll learn about gopher menus and how to use them with Internet Explorer.

LESSON 13 ACCESSING GOPHER SERVERS

In this lesson, you'll learn about Gopher menus and how to use them with Internet Explorer.

UNDERSTANDING GOPHER

Gopher was developed at the University of Minnesota and named after the university's mascot, the gopher. The name gopher also provides us with a good clue as to how we use the technology. With gopher, you dig through a system of menus (called gopherspace) much as a gopher would dig through the earth.

Gopher is a first-generation browsing system based on hypertext technology applied to menus. It works a lot like the menu system we saw at Yahoo (refer to Lesson 11 if you haven't used Yahoo before). However, gopher differs from the World Wide Web in that no graphics are used, and only menus can be used. There are no hyperlinked documents in gopher. A menu item can point to a document, but the document can't point anywhere.

CONNECTING TO A GOPHER SITE

Back in Lesson 1, I showed how Internet Explorer can use different protocols to transfer information from a remote computer to the computer on your desk. I also introduced the three main protocols that Internet Explorer can use:

- HTTP For transferring World Wide Web documents
- gopher For transferring gopher information
- ftp For transferring files

In this case, we'll use the gopher:// protocol instead of the http:// protocol. Other than that, the process is pretty much the same. For example, to view a document from the University of Missouri Web server, I type **http://showme.missouri.edu**. To view a menu from the University of Missouri Gopher server, I type **gopher://showme.missouri.edu**. Internet Explorer figures out all the rest.

Let's try a quick example:

1. Open the File menu and select the Open command. You will see the Open Internet Address dialog box.
2. Type **gopher://gopher.micro.umn.edu** and press Enter. After a few moments, you will see the University of Minnesota main gopher menu, as shown in Figure 13.1.

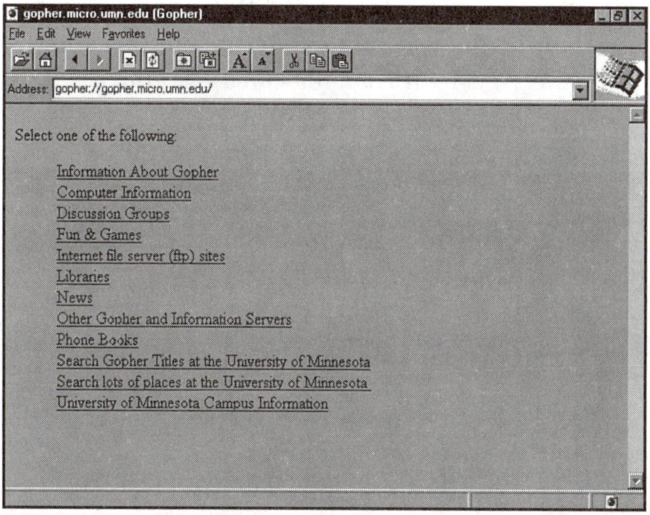

FIGURE 13.1 The University of Minnesota main Gopher menu.

3. To view a submenu on the gopher server, click the title of the item. Notice that menus are underlined in blue just like the hypertext of a Web document.

TIP **No Need for gopher://** If the name of the site begins with gopher (as in **gopher.micro.umn.edu**), you don't have to type the gopher://. Internet Explorer will automatically add that in for you.

MOVING THROUGH THE MENUS

Internet Explorer makes it a breeze to use gopher menus. As in the previous example, all you need to do is click a menu to view the next level down. Let's try another example using the Library of Congress gopher server:

1. Open the File menu and select the Open command. You should see the Open Internet Address dialog box.
2. Type **gopher://marvel.loc.gov** and press Enter. After a few moments, you will see the Library of Congress (LOC) main gopher menu, as shown in Figure 13.2.

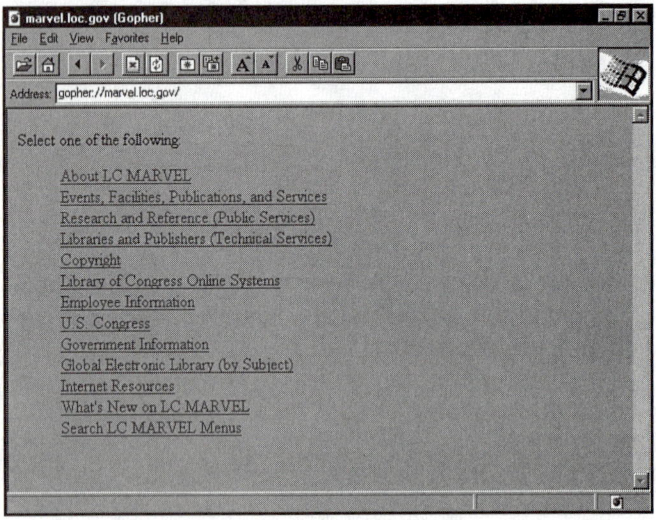

FIGURE 13.2 The Library of Congress main gopher menu.

3. Click the Government Information link. After a few moments, you should see another menu.
4. Click the Federal Information Resources link. After a few moments, you will see another menu.
5. Click the Information by Branch of Federal Government link. After a few moments, you will see another menu.
6. Click the Executive Branch link. After a few minutes, you will see another menu.
7. Click the White House link. After a few minutes, you will see another menu.
8. Click the Israeli-Palestine Peace Accord Remarks link. You will see the President's remarks to the Israeli-Palestine Peace Accord back in 1993.

Feel free to browse through the Library of Congress Gopher server, if this sort of information interests you. This archive contains thousands of fascinating documents, speeches, and reports. Use the Back button on the toolbar to get back to the main gopher menu.

As you can see, gopher is a useful tool. Although it's not as pretty as the World Wide Web, you can find all kinds of great information with gopher:

- Government documents, speeches, political papers, and study reports
- University research papers, statistics, and catalogs
- Local information on restaurants, movies, and other areas of entertainment
- Anything that anybody else decides to put on a gopher server
- Links to Telnet sites that contain MUDs and MOOs

> **Telnet** the Internet's oldest tool, is completely text-based. Telnet allows you access to mainframe computers from your PC; you may also be able to run some text-based programs on those mainframes. MUDs (Multi-User Dimensions or Dungeons, or Multi-User Dialogue) or MOOs (MUDs Object Oriented) allow you to play "virtual reality" text-based adventure games. Despite their lack of graphics, hundreds of MUDs still exist on the Internet. Check out the Mud Connector page at **http://www.radzone.org/mud/** to jump into some MUD.

SAVING GOPHER DOCUMENTS

With Internet Explorer, saving information you find with gopher couldn't be easier. Let's save the movie listing we saw in the previous example:

If you don't see the Movie Reviews, use the example above to get there. Then...

1. Open the File menu and select the Save As command. You should see the Save As dialog box.
2. Use the window to get the directory in which you'd like to save your document.
3. In the File Name edit field, type a name for your document.
4. To save the document, click Save.

If you'd like to start browsing around with gopher, I'd recommend you start at **gopher://gopher.micro.umn.edu** and go from there.

In this lesson, you learned about Gopher menus and how to use them with Internet Explorer.

In the next lesson, you'll learn about anonymous FTP and how to use it with Internet Explorer.

LESSON 14

Accessing Anonymous FTP Servers

In this lesson, you'll learn about anonymous FTP and how to use it with Internet Explorer.

Understanding Anonymous FTP

Back in Lesson 1, I told you about FTP, or File Transfer Protocol. This protocol, or computer language, allows the user to transfer files to and from a remote computer, a very handy thing.

Most FTP programs look like File Manager, with a list of files and directories and buttons you can use to copy them to your local computer. However, Internet Explorer has a slightly different look to it. If you've used FTP before, you'll see what I mean. If you haven't, don't worry. Learning to use it is quite simple.

Most FTP sites use an anonymous user ID. Anonymous means you don't need a user ID or password to get files from the site. If a site does not support anonymous FTP, you will not be able to use Internet Explorer to access it. Likewise, if you need to specify a user ID to get access to the files you need, Internet Explorer will not be able to help you. You'll need to use a Windows FTP client such as WS FTP. For more information on using FTP, consider reading Que's *10 Minute Guide to the Internet*.

Connecting to Anonymous FTP Sites

As with the other protocols supported by Internet Explorer, FTP sites require the use of an URL. It follows the same pattern as the gopher URL or the World Wide Web URL, but uses the ftp://

protocol instead. Here's an example of the URL I would use to get to the Microsoft FTP site:

ftp://ftp.microsoft.com/deskapps

Notice that I've specified a specific directory, deskapps. This URL would give me a list of all the files in the deskapps directory. Let's give it a try:

1. Open the File menu and select the Open command. You will see the Open Internet Address dialog box.
2. Type **ftp://ftp.microsoft.com/deskapps** and press Enter. After a few moments, you will see a screen similar to the one shown in Figure 14.1.

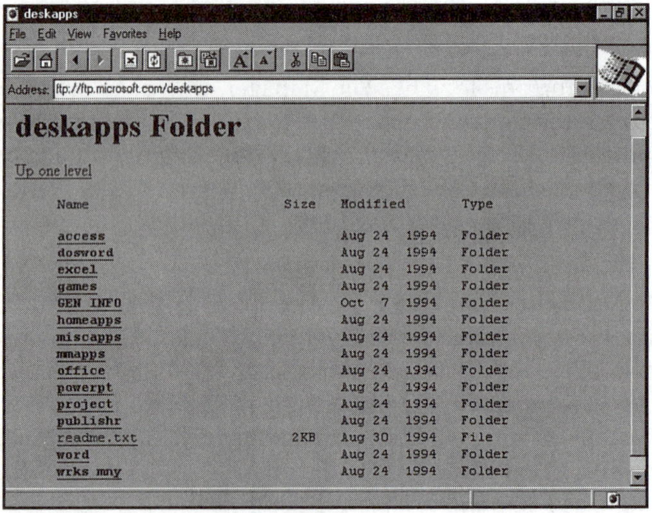

FIGURE 14.1 The Microsoft FTP site.

Directories in the list are shown with a bold typeface and have no number in the Size column, whereas files will have a number under the Size column. Only one file exists here, readme.txt.

To change directories, click the name of the directory. They act just like hypertext you're familiar with.

TIP **What's the Domain Name?** In many cases, though not all, you can figure out the domain name of an FTP server from the Web server URL—change the **www** to **ftp**. Using Microsoft as an example, change **www.microsoft.com** to **ftp.microsoft.com**. You'll also want to change the protocol to **ftp://**.

MOVING THROUGH THE DIRECTORIES

FTP sites run from a number of the different operating systems on the Internet, not just DOS or Windows. Therefore, you'll see some filenames and directory listings that don't look very familiar. Fortunately, though, Internet Explorer makes the whole thing a breeze. You won't even know you're accessing a different operating system on the other end.

For the most part, you'll only need to know three pieces of information about a directory listing, regardless of the operating system on the remote system:

- Is the entry a file or directory?
- What is the name of the file or directory?
- If the entry is a file, how big is it?

If you can get this information from the directory, you'll do just fine. Once you're connected, you'll want to do one of two things: change directories or download files. Changing directories is simple:

1. Open the File menu and select the Open command. You will see the Open Internet Address dialog box.
2. Type **ftp://ftp.microsoft.com** and press Enter. After a few moments, you should see the main FTP directory at Microsoft, as shown in Figure 14.2.

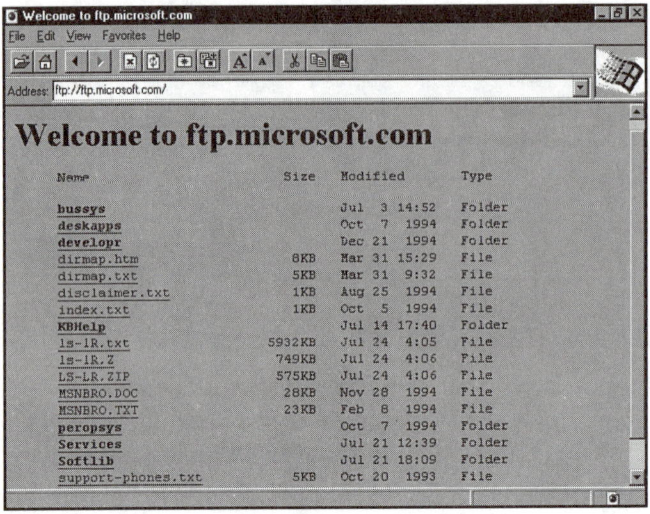

FIGURE 14.2 The Microsoft main FTP directory.

3. Click peropsys to change to the peropsys (Personal Operating System) directory. Your screen should resemble the one shown in Figure 14.3.

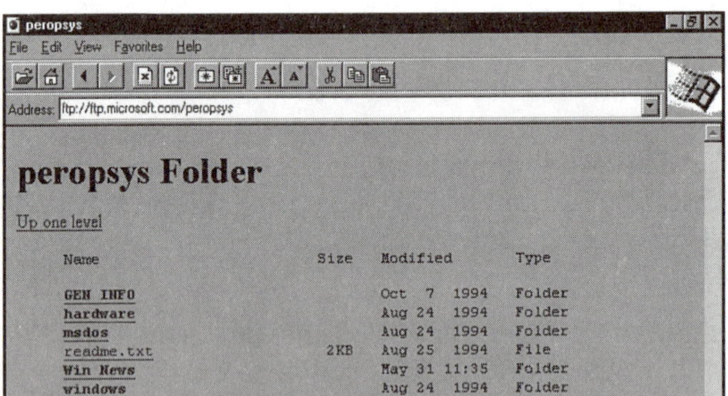

FIGURE 14.3 The peropsys directory.

4. Click windows to change to the windows directory. Your screen should resemble the one shown in Figure 14.4.

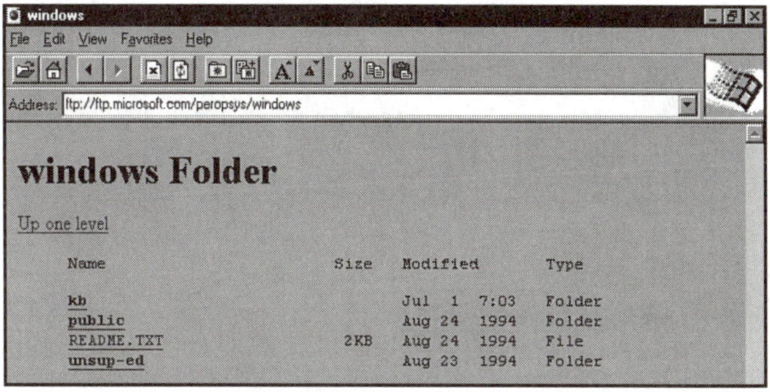

FIGURE 14.4 The windows directory.

5. Click public to change to the public directory. Your screen should resemble the one shown in Figure 14.5.

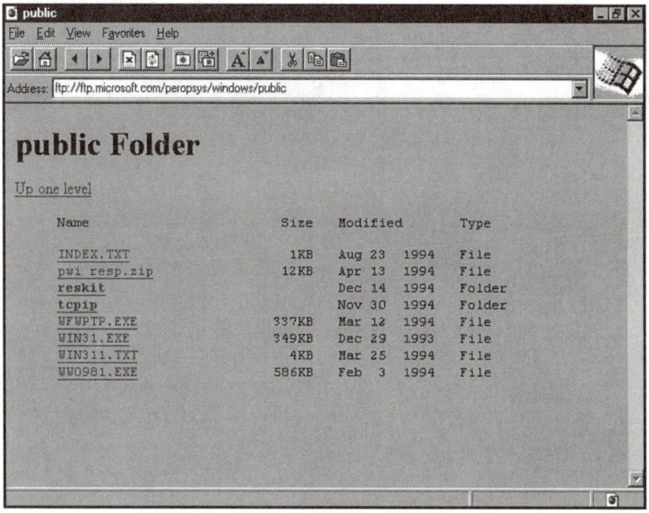

FIGURE 14.5 The public directory.

Back vs. Up One Level The Up One Level link is different from the Back button on the toolbar. The Back button will take you to the previously viewed page *which may not necessarily be up one level from the current FTP directory.* In most cases, they will act the same, but if you've come into an FTP directory via another link, they may act differently.

DOWNLOADING FILES

Downloading is just about as easy as changing directories, but you'll have a few more choices in some cases. First, you'll want to understand that the FTP part of Internet Explorer will attempt to open any file you click. By default, if the file is executable (or a .ZIP compressed file), Internet Explorer will ask you if you want to open it right away or just save it for now.

I would recommend saving the files first, then running them through a virus scanner (if you have one) before running or extracting them. It is generally best to avoid extracting .ZIP files or running .EXE files during a browsing session. Text files and document files will automatically load; you won't be prompted like you will for .ZIP and .EXE files.

TIP **What To Look For** When you browse through an FTP site, you'll notice that there are no descriptions for the files. How do you know what to download? Each directory will usually contain a file called **index** or **readme** or **readme.txt** or **index.txt** or something similar. Look for **index** or **readme**. Click that file to view a list of the files and a description for each one.

Let's go through a sample file download. I'm assuming you won't want to keep this file, so I'll take you to the point where you would download it, but I won't save it to your computer.

1. Open the File menu and select the Open command. You should see the Open Internet Address dialog box.
2. Type **ftp://ftp.microsoft.com/peropsys/windows/public** and press Enter. After a few moments, you should see the public directory, as just shown in Figure 14.5.
3. Click INDEX.TXT to view the README.TXT file. This text file, which will appear in your window, gives you some information about what's available in this directory.
4. After you've read the README.TXT file, click the back arrow on the toolbar. This will take you back to the public directory.
5. Click pwi_resp.zip to download the pwi_resp.zip file. You should see the Confirm File Open dialog box, as shown in Figure 14.6.

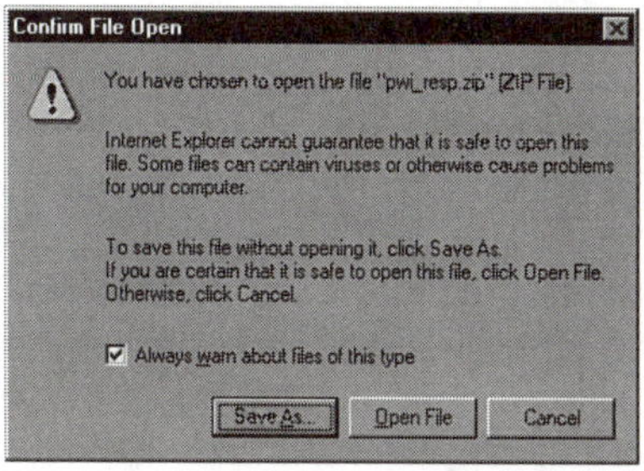

FIGURE 14.6 The Confirm File Open dialog box.

6. If you want to save the file, click Save As to save it. If not (you probably don't need this file) click Cancel.

In this lesson, you learned about anonymous FTP and how to use it with Internet Explorer.

In the next lesson, you'll learn how to view graphics files with Internet Explorer and save them if you want to keep them.

Lesson 15 Viewing and Saving Graphics Files

In this lesson, you'll learn how to view graphics files with Internet Explorer and how to save them if you want to keep them.

Viewing Graphics Files

Most of the Web pages we've looked at so far contain graphics of some kind or another. Most of the time, these graphics are in one of two formats:

- GIF GIF (pronounced "jif") stands for Graphics Interchange Format. It is a service mark of CompuServe. Many BBS and Internet sites will save graphics in this format since it is widely used and accepted as a graphics compression standard. These graphics are saved with a 256-color (8 bit) resolution. These files will have a .GIF extension.
- JPEG JPEG (pronounced "jay peg") stands for Joint Photography Experts Group. This format, which compresses more than GIF also boasts a 16.7 million-color (24 bit) resolution. These files will have a .JPG or .JPEG extension. If you have a 256-color video adapter (most people do), Internet Explorer will dither, or approximate, the colors for you, but the graphics may look a bit grainy.

Dither To dither means to "create" colors by using a group of similar colors. In lower color resolutions like 16 or 256 colors, images can't be displayed using all of their colors. Therefore, an application will use clusters of similar colors to give you the impression of the original color. This process is pretty effective, but causes a picture to look grainy.

With Internet Explorer, you'll get built-in support for both of these types of graphics. Virtually all graphics on the World Wide Web are in one of these two formats. If you run into graphics in other formats, you'll need to have another application on your hard disk to view them. For more information on viewing graphics on the Net, consider reading *Graphics on the Net* from Que, which will be out in October 1995.

Since Internet Explorer has built-in support for these two graphics formats, you can use it as a graphics viewer. And, like the rest of Internet Explorer, it's quite simple.

Since I'm not sure what graphics files you have on your computer, it's difficult to provide an actual example. I will, however, give you the steps to follow:

1. Open the File menu and select the Open command. You will see the Open Internet Address dialog box as shown in Figure 15.1.
2. Click Open File. You will see the Open File dialog box as shown in Figure 15.2.
3. From the File Types drop-down listbox, select All Files (*.*).
4. Change to the directory that contains the graphics file you wish to view.
5. Double-click the graphics file you wish to view. Internet Explorer will display that file in the window.

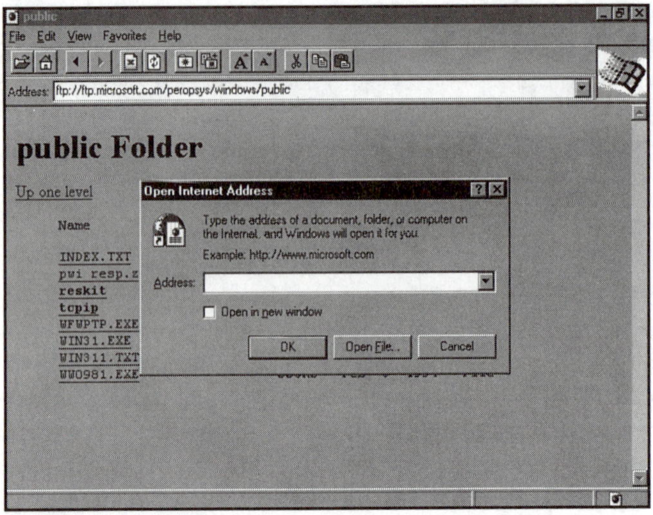

FIGURE 15.1 The Open Internet Address dialog box.

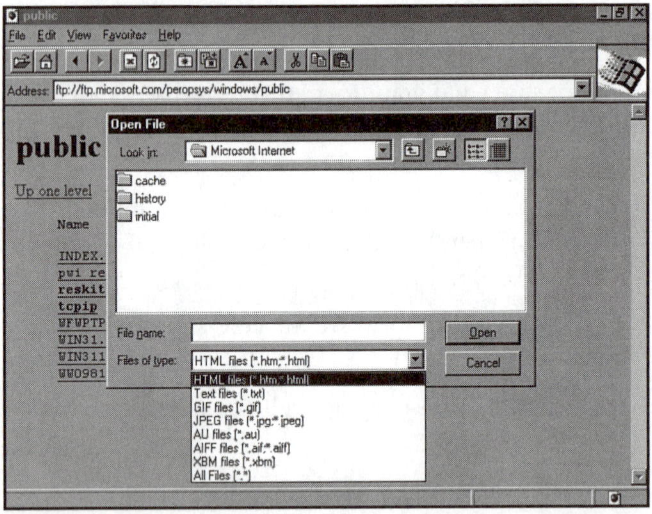

FIGURE 15.2 The Open File dialog box.

> If you don't have any graphics files on your hard disk, you won't be able to view any. This example assumes that you've saved, at some point in the past, a .GIF or .JPG file. Of course, you can't edit graphics files with Internet Explorer, but you can, at least, look at them.

SAVING GRAPHIC IMAGES

There are several ways to save the graphics you see in your Web pages. I'll show you how to use the three most convenient ways. With Internet Explorer, you can:

- Save a copy of an individual picture or graphic in a Web page.
- Save a copy of the image or pattern used as the background for a Web page.
- Drag and drop graphics from Internet Explorer onto your desktop, into another application, or into another document.

USING THE RIGHT MOUSE BUTTON

Internet Explorer provides quick and easy right-click access to many functions within Internet Explorer. To save a graphic you see in a Web page:

1. Place your mouse pointer over the graphic and right-click. You will see the menu shown in Figure 15.3.
2. Select the Save Picture As command. You will see the Save As dialog box.
3. In the window, change to the directory in which you'd like to save the graphic.

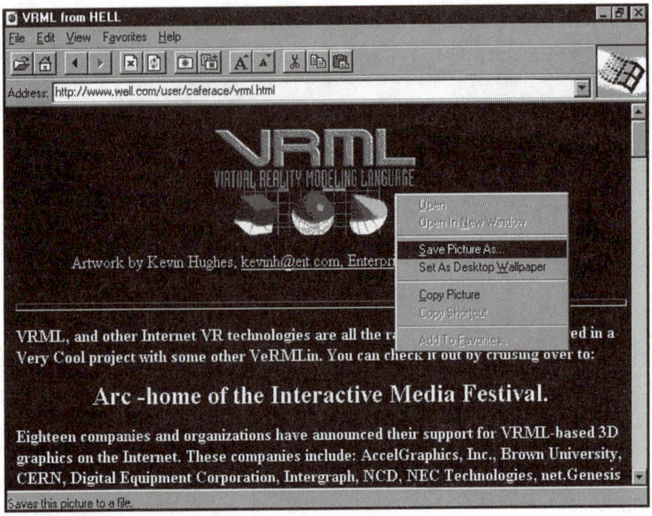

FIGURE 15.3 Saving a graphics file.

4. In the File Name edit field, type a name for the graphics file if you don't wish to use the name Internet Explorer provided for you.
5. To save the graphics file, click Save.

   If you'd rather save the graphic to the Clipboard (perhaps you'd like to paste it into another document), use the Copy Picture command instead.

COPYING AND SAVING BACKGROUND GRAPHICS

Some Web pages on the World Wide Web use backgrounds to enhance their appearance. Internet Explorer gives you the ability to capture those backgrounds or save them to a file for later use.

If you're not familiar with backgrounds, let's try a quick example:

1. Open the File menu and select the Open command. You will see the Open Internet Address dialog box.

2. Type **http://batmanforever.com/claw/claw.html** and press Enter. After a few moments, you will see the Riddler's home page as shown in Figure 15.4.

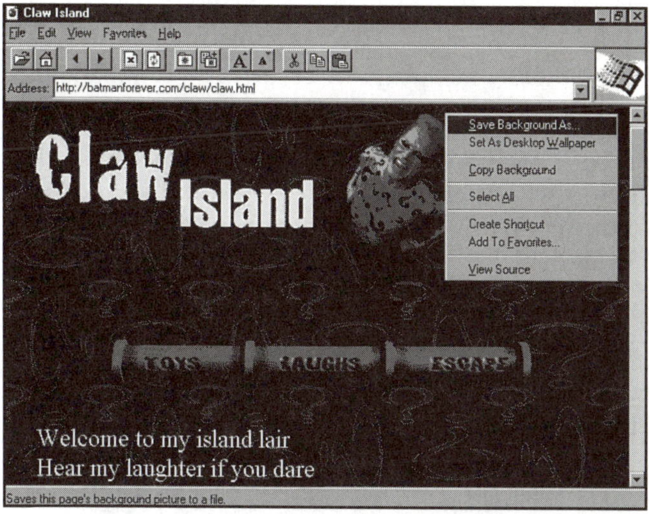

FIGURE 15.4 Saving the background.

Notice the pattern of question marks in the background. This pattern is a small .GIF file that is repeated over and over in a tiled fashion. To capture this image (or any other background image you wish to save)

1. Place your mouse pointer so it is not over any text or graphic, but over only the background of the document and right-click. You will see a small menu.

2. To copy the background image to the Clipboard, select the Copy Background command. To save the image to a file, select the Save Background As command. To use the background as your Windows 95 wallpaper, select the Set As Desktop Wallpaper command.

USING DRAG-AND-DROP

This method of saving graphics files is my favorite. Let's go back to the SOCKET Internet Services page, and drag and drop the SOCKET logo to the Desktop. From there, we can view it again later without having to go back online. Here's how:

1. Open the File menu and select the Open command. You will see the Open Internet Address dialog box.
2. Type **http://the-tech.mit.edu/Shakespeare** and press Enter. After a few moments, you will see the Complete Works of William Shakespeare page as shown in Figure 15.5.
3. Place your mouse pointer over the photograph of Shakespeare.
4. Click and hold down the mouse button, and drag your mouse pointer over to your Desktop.

FIGURE 15.5 The Complete Works of William Shakespeare page.

5. Release the mouse button to create a copy of the graphic image on your Desktop.
6. **(Optional)** To test the process, shut down Internet Explorer.
7. **(Optional)** Double-click the graphic icon on your Desktop. You will see Internet Explorer appear with the photograph of Shakespeare by itself in the window.

In this lesson, you learned how to view graphics files with Internet Explorer and how to save them if you want to keep them.

In the next lesson, you'll learn how to share information and data with other applications.

LESSON 16

Copying and Pasting Text and Links

In this lesson, you'll learn how to use drag-and-drop and other methods to share information and data with other applications. You'll also learn how to use other applications and accessories to share information with friends and colleagues.

Using Copy and Paste

When I use the Internet, I'm always running into some bit of information that makes me think, "I'd like to share this with John," or "Boy, Gary would really get a kick out of this." A way to copy information from a page would be great—without having to type it out, of course.

I've already shown you, back in Lesson 15, how to save the graphics from a page. Internet Explorer also provides a way to save the text from a page just as easily. This process is the same highlighting process used in other Windows programs, so you'll be used to doing this.

To demonstrate the copy-and-paste process, let's browse out to the SOCKET Internet Services page and copy the first sentence into an e-mail document. For this example, we'll use Microsoft Exchange, though any Windows e-mail application will work.

TIP Internet Explorer allows you to send e-mail while at a Web page. You may have already noticed that most Web pages have a "feedback" URL or address where you can contact that site; these links are highlighted just like normal hypertext. Many of them are an actual address—for example, **webmaster@mcp.com** at the Macmillan Publishing site. When you click on one of these links, Internet Explorer will automatically bring up Microsoft Exchange. If you need help configuring your e-mail, consult Que's *Using Microsoft Internet Explorer*.

1. Open the File menu and select the Open command. You will see the Open Internet Address dialog box.
2. Type **http://www.socketis.net** and press Enter. After a few moments, you will see the SOCKET Internet Services home page.
3. Using Figure 16.1 as a guide, place your pointer in front of the sentence under the graphic.

FIGURE 16.1 The SOCKET home page.

4. Hold down the left mouse button and drag the mouse to the end of the sentence. You should see a highlighted sentence as shown in Figure 16.2.

Do not click on the hyperlink to highlight it; it won't work. You'll need to start with either regular text or click on the background in front of or above the hyperlink. Also, if the sentence you are trying to highlight contains a hyperlink, you may notice that the hyperlink may highlight in a different color. Don't worry, the text of the hyperlink will still copy.

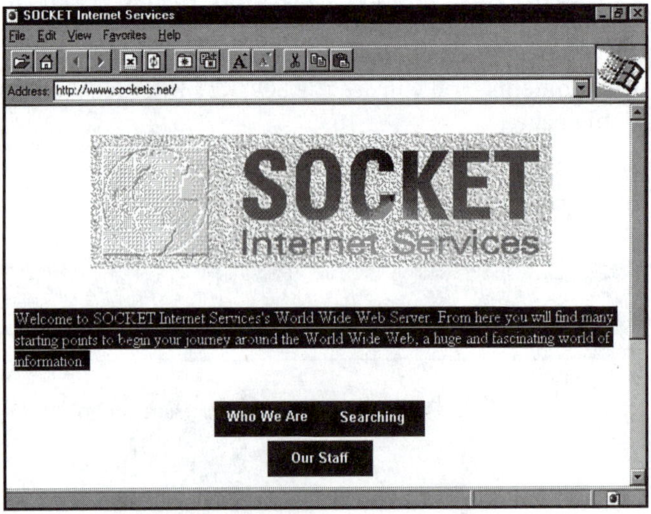

FIGURE 16.2 Highlighted text.

5. Open the Edit menu and select the Copy command.

The text has been copied to the Windows Clipboard, an area of memory used to exchange data between programs. If you want to paste this information into another application, the process is just as simple. We'll assume that Microsoft Exchange is configured correctly on your computer; consult *Using Microsoft Internet Explorer* from Que if you need help.

> TIP **I Want To Copy All of It.** If you want to select the entire document, press Ctrl+A. The entire text of the document will be selected; then you can use the Copy command to copy the entire document to the Clipboard.

1. Double-click the Microsoft Exchange icon on your desktop. It's the one showing three standing envelopes.
2. Click on the New Message icon or choose Compose, New Message.
3. Place the cursor inside the message box.
4. To paste your text into this application, open the Edit menu and select the Paste command. The text will appear as shown in Figure 16.3. Alternatively, use the Paste icon.

If you want to send your message, type in an e-mail address in the To: box and select File, Send—or click on the Send icon.

> TIP **Keyboard Shortcuts!** You can save a little time by using Ctrl+C to copy and Ctrl+V to paste. This works in any Windows application.

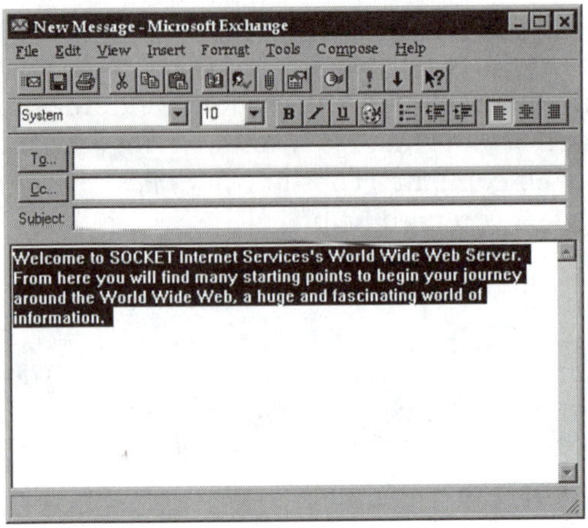

FIGURE 16.3 A sentence pasted into an e-mail message.

COPYING HYPERLINKS TO THE CLIPBOARD

You might also run across a cool link that you'd like to share with your friends. I do this all the time at work; while I'm doing some research, I'll stumble onto something that doesn't really help me all that much, but I know that a colleague could benefit from the information.

In the past, I've had to type out the URL (or even write it down), and send it to my colleague. Now, I can drag the link into a mail message and send it off. With the first method, the other person would either have to type the URL in manually, or copy and paste it into an Open URL dialog box to get to the page. With Internet Explorer, the other person simply double-clicks an icon and Internet Explorer opens up and retrieves the document.

So, how does all this work? Well, the first part is quite simple. Let's use a quick example from the Microsoft home page:

1. Open the File menu and select the Open command. You should see the Open Internet Address dialog box.
2. Type **http://www.microsoft.com** and press Enter. After a few moments, you should see the Microsoft home page.
3. Place your pointer over a hypertext link (there should be one labeled Microsoft Products, but they change it often) and right-click. You should see a small menu as shown in Figure 16.4 below.

FIGURE 16.4 Select the Copy Shortcut command.

4. Select the Copy Shortcut command to copy the URL to the Windows Clipboard.

Now that you've copied the URL to the Clipboard, you can paste it into another document or send it to a friend. You can use the Paste Shortcut command in any Windows application that supports the use of shortcuts. These include, but are not limited to:

- Microsoft Exchange This is where I most often use Internet Explorer shortcuts. The recipient of my e-mail can double-click the shortcut in the e-mail message to automatically browse to that Web page.
- Desktop You can paste these shortcuts to your Desktop, as well. If you have a Web page you'd like to look at frequently, paste it to the Desktop. To view it again later, double-click the shortcut. Internet Explorer will automatically start and retrieve the document from the Web.

Not all applications and programs support shortcuts. You might think that the URL as text is in the Clipboard, but that's not the case. Generally, if the program won't give you the Paste Shortcut command, you can't paste the shortcut.

USING DRAG-AND-DROP

This method of copying shortcuts is my favorite. It works the same way as with graphics (Lesson 15 shows you how to drag and drop graphics from a Web page), and it's a bit easier than using the cut-and-paste method I discussed in the previous section. I'll use the Desktop as an example. To drag and drop a shortcut from a Web page to the Desktop

1. Make sure you can see part of the Desktop behind the Internet Explorer window. If you can't, you'll want to move the Internet Explorer window out of the way—if it's maximized, you'll need to unmaximize (restore) the window first.
2. Place your mouse pointer over any hypertext link (Internet Explorer calls them shortcuts). You should see the pointer change to a hand.
3. Hold down your mouse button and drag your mouse cursor to the desktop. You will see the mouse cursor change into an arrow with a box and a + sign. This indicates that information is to be copied to this location.
4. Release the mouse button to copy the shortcut to the desktop.

To view this document later, double-click the icon on the desktop. Internet Explorer will automatically start (if it's not loaded already) and display the Web page associated with that shortcut.

In this lesson, you learned how to use drag-and-drop and other methods to share information and data with other applications. You've also learned how to use other applications and accessories to share information with friends and colleagues.

In the next lesson, you'll learn about the dangers of shopping and online transactions with Internet Explorer.

Lesson 17 Shopping with Internet Explorer

In this lesson, you'll learn about the do's and don'ts of shopping on the Internet. You'll also learn about some cool places to do some shopping.

Understanding Internet Security

Understandably, people get nervous when a form on the Internet asks for a credit-card number. How is this information being used? Who else has access to it? Can I be cheated? Unfortunately, it's hard to tell. You have to be careful.

There are a few ways to deal with the security problem.

- Take a risk. After all, whenever you pass out your credit card to a waiter, or read the number over the phone, you are risking being the victim of fraud. Is the Internet more risky than such transactions? Probably not. And anyway, if you are ripped off (which is highly unlikely), the credit-card company will pay most, if not all, of the loss.
- Only work with sites that use some form of secure "money," such as sites that work with First Virtual accounts.
- Only shop at sites that you can set up an account with; you call them on the phone and give them your credit-card number. In return you get an account number that you can use to buy. Is this safer than using a credit card in the first place? Probably not, but it keeps some people happy.

- Don't use Internet Explorer to shop online. Some Web browsers (in particular Netscape) use a form of encryption that secures your data as it is transferred over the Internet, so no one can intercept the data and use it. Internet Explorer has no support for security encryption.

You should note that it usually doesn't matter if you don't have a browser that works with an encryption system. The Netscape system, for instance, only works if you use Netscape to connect to a site that is using the Netscape https:// server. But most commercial sites are not using these servers, so it matters not one whit which browser you are using when you connect to such sites. That is, if you connect to a non-https:// server using Netscape, your transaction will be no more secure than if you use Internet Explorer.

Also, note that many of the online "shopping" areas are nothing of the sort. Many, perhaps most, are online advertising areas; you can't order online, you have to order through an 800 number. The hype about online shopping has most definitely outrun the reality.

This doesn't mean you can't shop with Internet Explorer; you'll just want to make a phone call instead of placing an order online, or set up a First Virtual account so you can order completely online.

FINDING COOL PLACES TO SHOP

The World Wide Web is filled with online malls, online mail-order houses, online catalogs, online whatever else you can think of. You'll also find that many businesses provide Web pages that allow you to peruse their products and services and even place an order online.

In addition to the many URLs in Appendix A, here are some great places to start if you're looking for stuff to buy online.

- Go to the Yahoo search page (**http://www.yahoo.com/search.html**) and search for shopping.

- Go to the WebCrawler (**http://www.webcrawler.com**), set the number of hits to return to 500 and search for shopping. Yes, you'll get the first 500 out of about 2,500 Internet shopping sites that WebCrawler has found so far.

These two sites can usually get you all the information you could ever want about online shopping.

For an example of an online mall, see Figure 17.1. This is Shopping2000 (**http://shopping2000.com/shopping2000/**), a large mall that lets you buy everything from flowers to art, cars to books.

FIGURE 17.1 Shopping2000, a large Internet mall.

MAKING A PURCHASE ONLINE

Many of the Web sites you'll run into on the Internet will give you the power to make a purchase online. In most cases, you'll have to provide a credit-card number, or maybe a First Virtual account ID. As with making a purchase over the telephone, if you make a purchase online, keep track of the following information:

- The name of the organization from which you made the purchase.
- The URL of the site from which you shopped. This information is traceable and can be used to track down somebody who has taken advantage of you or abused your credit-card number.
- The merchandise you purchased, and the cost. Criminals who engage in credit-card fraud will often provide legitimate merchandise for a reasonable price, then drastically overcharge your credit card.
- If you feel suspicious but you still want to make the purchase, print out a copy of the screen (or take a screen shot).

Note that some shopping sites won't allow you to order online. They simply refer you to an 800 number. Others won't take your order unless you've set up an account with them first (again, by calling their 800 line and getting an account number). Others will let you send your credit-card number if you wish, or order online, or use some kind of account system. You'll run into a lot of variations. One of the most unusual is the Pizza Hut site (**http://www.pizzahut.com/**), which asks for no payment—see Figure 17.2. (You're going to pay the pizza delivery man when he arrives, after all!) Not all areas can order from Pizza Hut online, though.

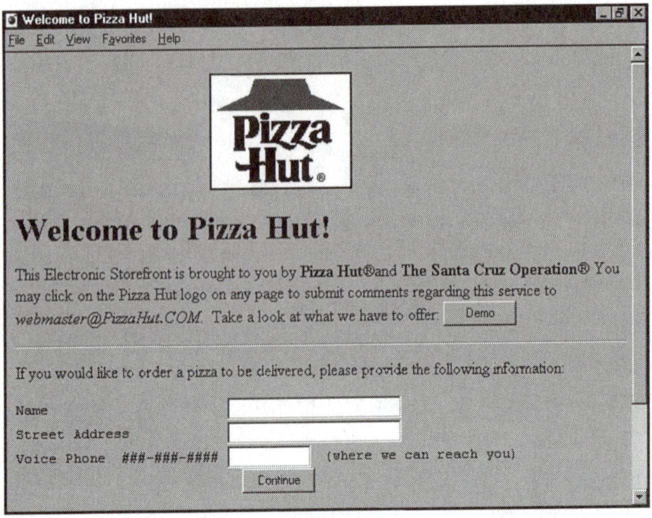

FIGURE 17.2 No payment's required at the Pizza Hut site.

IF YOU WANT TO BE SAFE

Let's take a quick look at several ways to secure your transactions: First Virtual, Netcash, and ecash. These systems allow you to set up an account, or obtain "net money," and then go shopping. The drawback is that most sites you'll find don't use systems like this. (Most just use the telephone!) Still, their popularity may grow, and in the not-so-distant future you may find them essential.

FIRST VIRTUAL

You can reach First Virtual at **http://firstvirtual.com/** (see Figure 17.3). It's very simple to set up an account; here's how it works. First, you apply for an account. You can do so from links at the First Virtual site that takes you to a form, or an e-mail window, or a Telnet site (the link opens Windows Telnet). You'll enter information such as your name and address, e-mail address, an account ID you'd like to use, and so on.

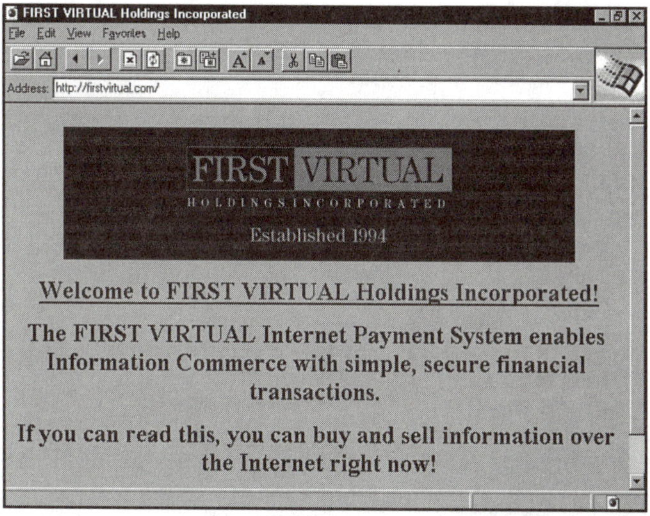

FIGURE 17.3 Setting up an Internet shopping account.

A little later, you'll get an e-mail message back from First Virtual. This message will contain a special number. You must then call an 800 number and ask to open an account; you'll provide the person answering with the special number from the e-mail message and your credit-card number. A little later (perhaps an hour or so), you'll receive another e-mail message, informing you that your account is ready to be used. There's a $2 fee for setting up an account, but no fee for using the account. (You'll have to reapply each time your credit card is reissued.)

How can you shop with your First Virtual account? Well, take a look at Figure 17.4. This is a form used to download Apple QuickTime for Windows, a program that plays QuickTime videos.

(You can get to this site at **http://quicktime.apple.com/order-qt2win.html**.) The very first box in this form is for your First Virtual account ID. When you enter all the information into the form and then click on the Purchase button, the information is transferred to Apple. They send the account number to First Virtual, asking for payment. First Virtual then sends you an e-mail message asking you to confirm that you really did make the purchase. No confirmation from you, no payment.

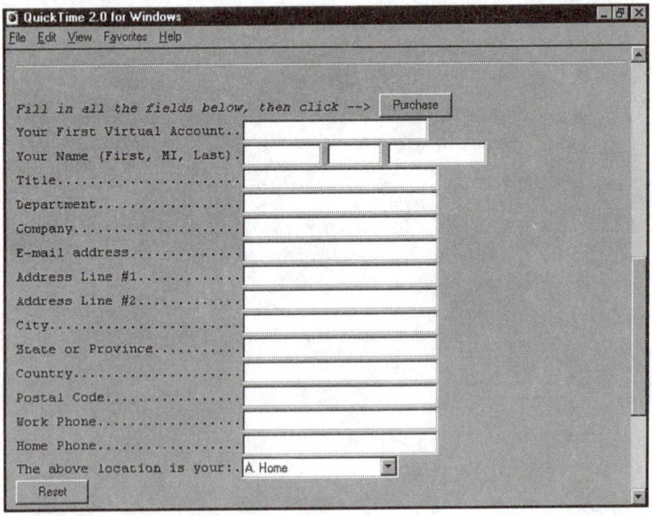

FIGURE 17.4 Downloading Apple QuickTime for Windows.

USING NETCASH

If First Virtual is the Internet's equivalent of a credit-card account, NetCash is the Internet's equivalent of cold, hard cash. It's a sort of virtual currency that can be used to purchase goods, services, and information over the Internet. Like paper currency, each "bill" or "coupon" has a value and a serial number. These serial numbers are unique to each coupon.

To acquire NetCash, go to **http://www.teleport.com/~netcash/ncquick.html**. The recommended way to get NetCash is using their "e-mail check-cashing service," which works like this. First, you fill out a form (you can see part of the form in Figure 17.5). You'll enter information about your checking account, including a check number, routing number, and account number, along with your driver's license number and social security number. (Seems to me you are giving away a lot of information in order to be more secure!)

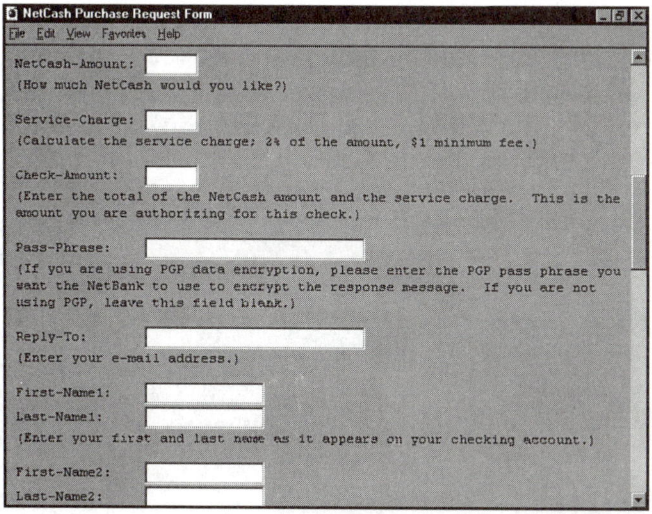

FIGURE 17.5 Getting online cash from NetCash.

After sending the form you get an e-mail message back, with a NetCash "coupon," like this:

NetCash US$ 25.00 A123456B789012C

The number at the end is the number you'll use when you buy something from an online merchant.

Pending vs. Valid When you first get this cash, it has a special status of "pending." Your information hasn't cleared the bank, after all. The NetCash people say that most merchants will accept "pending" cash, but some may not accept it until the status has changed to "valid" (which may take ten days). Or they may accept it but not ship until the status changes to "valid." So check before you buy.

Now, you are ready to buy. You will have to "send" the NetCash to the online store, either via e-mail or from a Web-page form. You can see in Figure 17.6, for instance, how to buy from Sound Wire using NetCash (**http://soundwire.com/**). You can also pay with a credit card or through a First Virtual account.

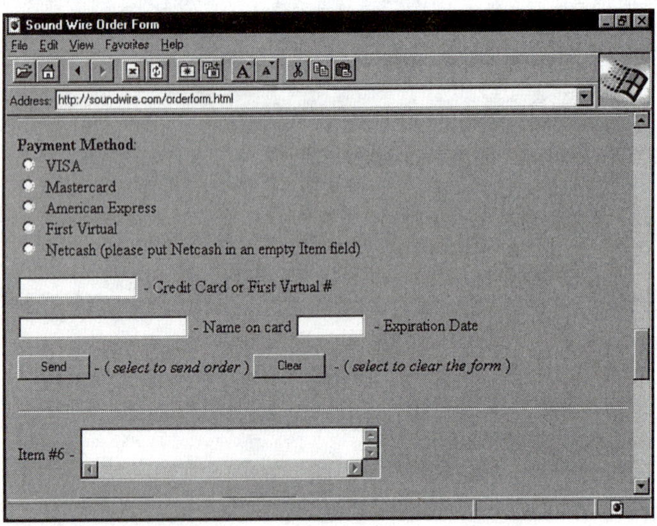

FIGURE 17.6 The Sound Wire site.

The obvious problem, though, is making change. After all, you may have a $25 coupon. What if you only want to spend $5? You can ask the NetCash bank to make change for you, by sending an e-mail message to the bank. For instance, you might send this message:

NetCash US$ 25.00 A123456B789012C /Change 5.00

And get the following message in return:

Total Pending: $ 25.00

NetCash US$ 20.00 B234567C890123D

NetCash US$ 5.00 C345678D901234E

Now you have two coupons, for $5 and $20.

There's a fee for using NetCash, by the way; 2 percent of the cash you buy, with a $1 minimum charge. There's no fee for making change. Currently only a few online stores use NetCash, but you can find a list of the ones that do at **http://www.teleport.com/~netcash/ncmerch.html**.

USING ECASH

There's another, similar system, called ecash (often also known as DigiCash, after the company that owns the system, and CyberBucks; all rather confusing). Again, there are only a few sites accepting this form of cash (you can see a list at **http://www.digicash.com/shops/cybershop.html**), but perhaps a few more than NetCash. Ecash has an unusual feature, though; you can use it to send money to anyone with an ecash account, not just stores. So you can send money to friends, family, or whomever else.

This system requires that you install a special program, the ecash client program, that helps you set up a special account at the ecash bank. When you want to use ecash, you use the program to withdraw "digital coins," which are stored on your hard disk.

The ecash program works like a viewer. When you are ready to use your money, the Web form you are working at will open the ecash program and ask you to confirm the transaction. Just click on Yes and the money is transferred to the online store. The "digital coins" are then transferred from your hard disk to the store. The ecash program encrypts the data before transferring it across the Internet, so it's secure.

For more information about ecash, go to **http://www.digicash.com/ecash/**.

By the way, if all this seems like a lot of trouble to buy something online, I have to agree with you. It's often easier just to pick up the phone!

In this lesson, you learned about the do's and don'ts of shopping on the Internet. You also learned about some cool places to do some shopping.

In the next lesson, you'll learn how to configure the appearance of Internet Explorer to match your tastes and preferences.

Lesson 18

Changing the Look of Internet Explorer

In this lesson, you'll learn how to configure the appearance of Internet Explorer to match your tastes.

You can do several things to change the appearance of Internet Explorer. You can configure the items that appear in the window, and you can change the appearance of the text, the background, and the hypertext link. You can also tell Internet Explorer whether or not to display technical information about shortcuts and hyperlinks on the status line. To speed things up, you can even prevent Internet Explorer from loading the graphics in a document.

To make it easier to use this book as reference later on, I'll include each option in its own section.

Adding or Removing Items from the Window

You can add or remove three different items from the Internet Explorer window:

- The toolbar
- The address bar
- The status line

If you're using a small monitor or your screen does not use a very high resolution, you may want to see more of your document. To do this, you can turn off the toolbar, address bar, and the status line, leaving more room for the document. Of course, you can always turn them back on again. To add or remove items from the window:

1. Open the View menu. You should see three selections: Toolbar, Address Bar and Status Line.
2. If the item has a check next to it, the item is currently displayed in the window. To remove the item, select it.
3. If the item does not have a check next to it, it is not currently displayed in the window. To add the item, select it.

As you can see, these commands act as a toggle; if the item is present, the command will remove it; if the item is not present, the command will add it.

Changing the Appearance of Text, Backgrounds, and Graphics

You can change the color of the text in your Web pages, change the default background for Web pages, and specify whether or not Internet Explorer will load the graphics in a document.

To change these options:

1. Open the View menu and select the Options command. You will see the Options dialog box, as shown in Figure 18.1.

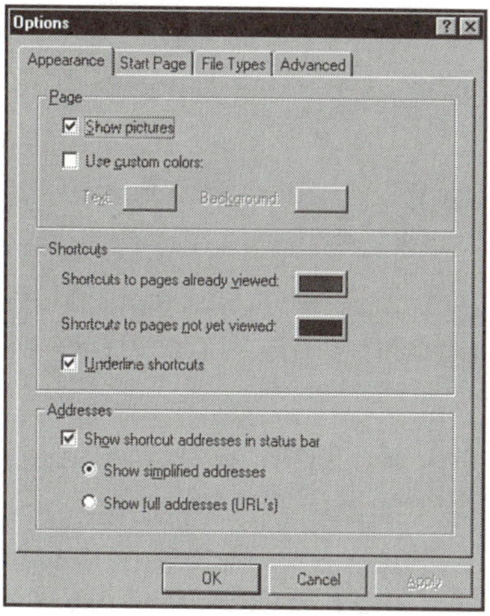

FIGURE 18.1 The Options dialog box.

2. If you want to prevent Internet Explorer from loading the graphics in a document (this can save lots of time), clear the check in the box labeled Show Pictures.
3. To use custom colors for the text and the background, check the box labeled Use Custom Colors. Notice that the two buttons underneath are no longer grayed out.
4. To change the color for the text or background, click the colored button next to the one you want to change.
5. Select a color from the palette of colors that appears and click OK.

> Custom backgrounds will *not* replace backgrounds on Web pages that use tiled backgrounds or specify a background color.

Changing the Color of Hyperlinks

You can also change the color of hyperlinks or shortcuts. To change the colors:

1. Open the View menu and select Options. You will see the Options dialog box, as shown in Figure 18.1.
2. The middle section, labeled Shortcuts, contains two buttons, one for shortcuts you've already visited, and one for shortcuts you haven't seen yet.
3. To change the color of one or the other, click on the button. You should see a palette of colors.
4. Click on the colors you'd like the shortcuts to be, then click OK. You are back at the Options dialog box.
5. Click OK to return to Internet Explorer.

Toggling Shortcuts on the Status Line

Internet Explorer, by default, will inform you of the file to which a shortcut will take you. Try it out:

1. Place your mouse cursor over any hyperlink.
2. Look at the status bar at the bottom of the window. It should read Shortcut to and then the filename.

If you want, Internet Explorer will display the entire URL instead of just the filename. Or you can turn the feature off altogether. To configure this option:

1. Open the View menu and select the Options command. You should see the Options dialog box, as shown in Figure 18.1.
2. In the bottom section, labeled Addresses, check the box to display shortcuts in the status bar.

3. If you've opted to display shortcuts on the status bar, decide whether you'd like to see the entire URL or just the filename.

4. If you'd like to see the entire URL, click Show Full Addresses. Otherwise, click Show Simplified Addresses.

CHANGING THE START PAGE

When you run Internet Explorer for the first time, you'll see the Microsoft home page. This page contains links to lots of great information, but you may find that you'd rather start with a different page. Changing this option is simple.

To change your start page or home page:

1. Open the File menu and select the Open command. You should see the Open Internet Address dialog box.

2. Type the URL of the page you'd like to set as your start page and press Enter. After a few moments, you should see the page in the window.

3. Open the View menu and select the Options command. You should see the Options dialog box.

4. Click the Start Page tab at the top of the dialog box. You should see the start page options.

5. Click Use Current to set the current document as your start page. If you change your mind after a while, click Use Default to set the start page back to the Microsoft home page.

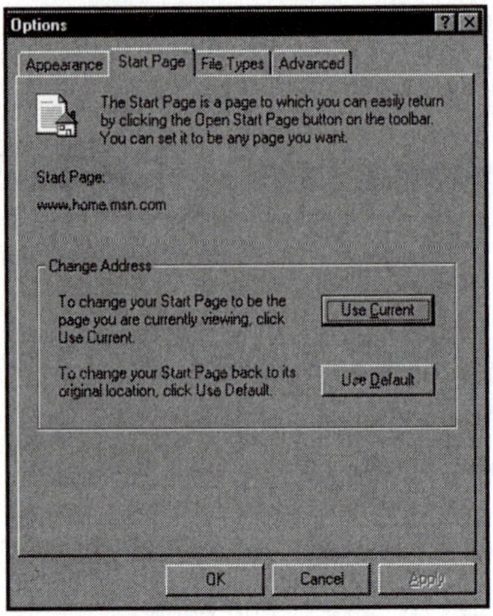

FIGURE 18.2 Configuring the Start Page.

In this lesson, you learned how to configure the appearance of Internet Explorer to match your tastes and preferences.

In the next lesson, you'll learn how to configure Internet Explorer to play sound if your machine has multimedia capabilities. You'll also learn about the different types of sound files often seen on the Internet.

Playing Internet Audio

LESSON 19

In this lesson, you'll learn how to configure Internet Explorer to play sound if your machine has multimedia capabilities. You'll also learn about the different types of sound files often seen on the Internet.

Setting Up Your Sound Card

Here's where Windows 95 is really cool. Normally, I'd have to provide a big, long description of how to configure your sound card, but Windows 95 configures it for you. How nice!

So, before we proceed, let's test the sound card to make sure it works OK. To find out whether you have support for sound installed, look at the right-hand side of your taskbar. You should see an icon of a yellow speaker, indicating that sound support is installed, running, and working properly.

If you don't see the icon, you need to do a more thorough check. If you see the icon, you can skip to the next section.

1. Double-click the My Computer icon on your desktop. You'll see the My Computer window.
2. Double-click the Control Panel icon. You'll see the Control Panel window.
3. Double-click the Multimedia icon. You'll see the Multimedia Properties dialog box.

4. Under the Audio tab, labeled Playback, you'll see the name of a sound card driver. If you see [None], you probably don't have a sound card. Consult your computer retailer for information on how to buy one.

If everything seems to be in order, we can make sure the sound card works. Windows 95 will usually copy some basic .WAV files to your system when your first install it. To play one of these .WAV files:

1. Click the Start button on your Taskbar. You'll see the main Start menu.
2. Select the Find menu. You'll see a submenu.
3. In the submenu, select Files or Folders. You'll see the Find dialog box, as shown in Figure 19.1.

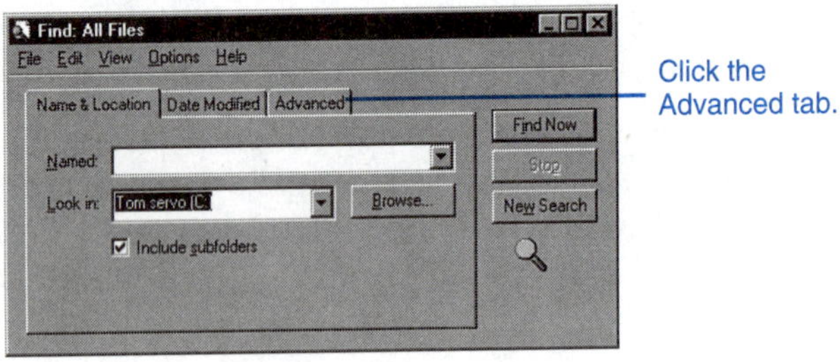

FIGURE 19.1 The Find dialog box.

4. Click the Advanced tab at the top of the dialog box. You'll see the advanced Find options.
5. In the dropdown list labeled Of Type:, select Wave Sound. Refer to Figure 19.2.
6. Click Find Now to locate the .WAV files on your system. A small window will appear beneath the Find dialog box.

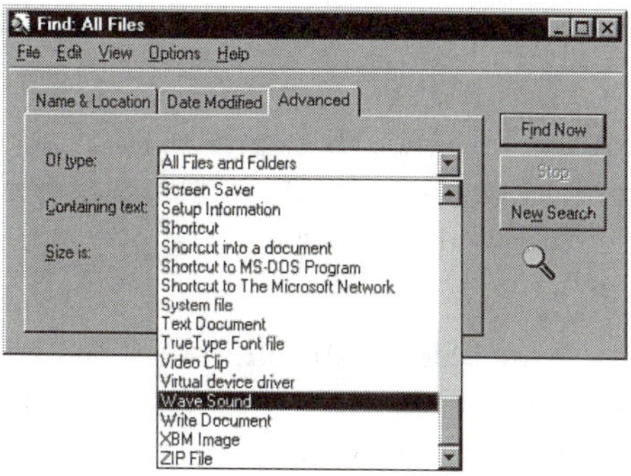

FIGURE 19.2 Searching for wave sounds on your computer.

If you have any .WAV files on your computer, they will appear in this box. Double-click any file that shows up in this list. If you hear a sound from your speakers, your sound card is working with Windows 95. If you see the error message shown in Figure 19.3, you won't be able to hear sounds on your machine.

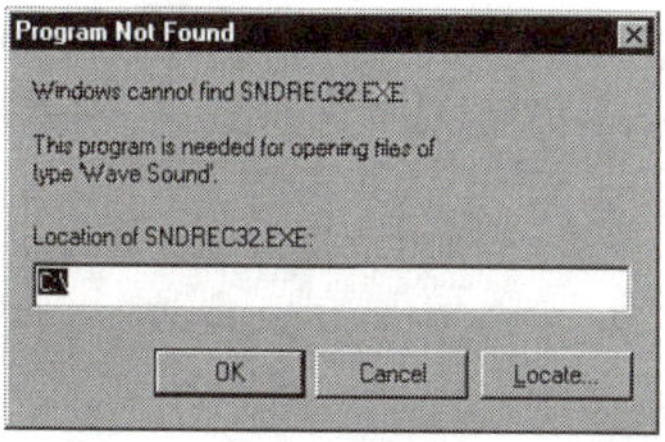

FIGURE 19.3 Windows can't find the program that plays sounds.

LEARNING SOUND FILE EXTENSIONS

Most of the sound files you'll run into on the Internet use one of the following formats:

- .AU These are AUdio files from the UNIX platform. Internet Explorer provides built-in support to play these files. You won't need to configure anything to get them to play.

- .AIF Also seen as .AIFF, these are UNIX-based files as well. Internet Explorer provides built-in support to play these files. You won't need to configure anything to get them to play.
- .SND These are Macintosh sound files that are not supported by Windows 95 or Internet Explorer. Because of technical differences in the way the Macintosh operating system works, files of this type must be prepared in a special way before they will work with a Windows 95 PC.
- .WAV These are Microsoft Wave files. These can be played on almost any system with a sound card. Windows 95 provides built-in support for playing these files, so you won't need to configure anything for these to work.
- .MID These are MIDI files. They do not contain digitized sound, but instead contain instructions for the computer to play a song with built-in sounds. Windows 95 will play .MID files also, so you don't have to configure a player for these, either.

> **These Files Can Be Quite Large!** Remember, sound files can be rather large, depending upon the quality of the recording, length of the sound, etc. If you're attempting to retrieve a sound file from the Internet over a modem, be prepared to practice your patience.

If you want to play .AIF, .AU, or .WAV files, you won't have to worry about a thing. However, you won't be able to play .SND files unless you install special software. Most of the software I've seen that plays .SND doesn't work very well, and it's usually very difficult to install. Also, you'd have to manually add the .SND file type to the Windows 95 Registry, which is also no small task. If you'd like a more in-depth guide to running different types of multimedia under Windows 95, consider reading *Special Edition Using Windows 95,* published by Que.

PLAYING SOUNDS FROM THE INTERNET

Occasionally, you'll run across a shortcut or hyperlink to a sound file on the Internet. You can usually click a shortcut or hyperlink to download a copy of the file and play it through Internet Explorer or Media Player. As I mentioned above, Media Player, which comes with Windows 95, will play .WAV files through your sound card, and Internet Explorer will play .AU files and .AIF files.

How do you know the shortcut points to a sound file? Usually, you'll only be able to tell from context, or the information surrounding the shortcut. When you click a shortcut to a sound file, Internet Explorer will retrieve the file and play it through your sound card. If you have a sound card, and it works, try this quick example:

1. Open the File menu and select the Open command. You will see the Open Internet Address dialog box.
2. Type **http://www.whitehouse.gov** and press Enter. After a few moments, you will see the White House home page, as shown in Figure 19.4.
3. The graphic you see is an image map. To hear a .WAV file of President Clinton, scroll down to the bottom icon labeled President's Welcome Message. You will see a choice of three formats, .AU, .WAV, and text.
4. Since Internet Explorer supports both .AU and .WAV, it doesn't matter which of the first two you choose. If you can't decide, choose the .WAV file. After a few moments, you will hear the sound.

Use the scroll bar to see the rest of the graphic.

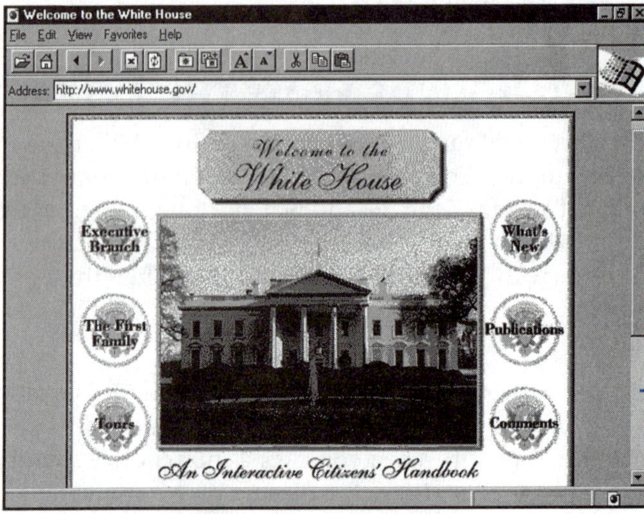

Figure 19.4 The White House home page.

There's also a new way to include sounds in a Web page on the Internet. It's called RealAudio. Instead of retrieving an entire file, then playing it (like the rest of the formats above), RealAudio allows your computer to play the sound *as it comes in from the Internet.* This process is much smoother and more efficient.

If you'd like information on how to do this, browse to **http://www.realaudio.com**.

Playing Sounds from Your Hard Disk

Since Internet Explorer has the capability to play all these different types of sound for you, you can use it to play sounds that are already on your hard disk.

The Media Player plays .WAV files, so if you'd like to hear a .WAV file, use that. If you'd like to hear a .AU or .AIF file, Internet Explorer will play it for you. To make it even easier, these file types will automatically run Internet Explorer if you double-click them. If you're already in Internet Explorer, and you'd like to play one of these files:

1. Open the File menu and select the Open command. You will see the Open Internet Address dialog box.
2. Click Open File. You will see a standard Open File dialog box, as shown in Figure 19.5.

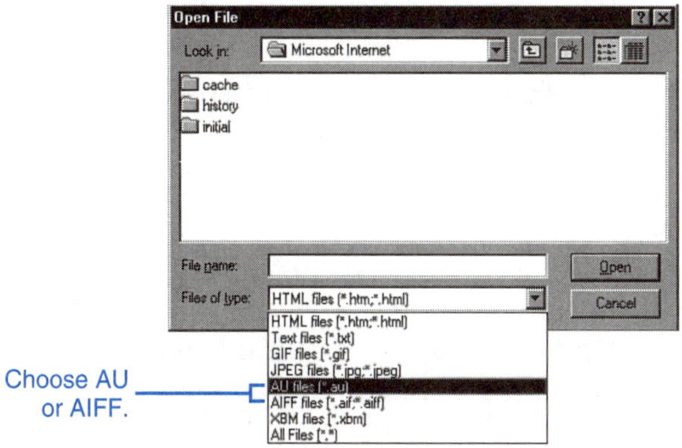

FIGURE 19.5 Loading a sound file.

3. In the dropdown list labeled Files of Type:, select either .AU Files or .AIF Files, depending on the type of file you wish to listen to.
4. In the window, browse to the directory that contains the sound file.
5. Double-click the name of the file to load it into Internet Explorer.

I Don't Have Any Sound Files! It's quite possible that, since .AU and .AIF files are UNIX files, you won't have any sound files on your computer.

TIP

Load Sound Files Quickly You can also use the Find Files or Folders command in the Start menu in your taskbar to look for .AU or .AIF files. If you find a sound file you want to hear, double-click it to load it into Internet Explorer.

In this lesson, you learned how to configure Internet Explorer to play sound if your machine has multimedia capabilities. You also learned about the different types of sound files often seen on the Internet.

In the next lesson, you'll learn how to configure Internet Explorer to play video and animation files, if your machine has multimedia capabilities. You'll also learn about the different types of video and animation files often seen on the Internet.

Playing Video and Animation Files

LESSON 20

In this lesson, you'll learn how to configure Internet Explorer to play video and animation files, if your machine has multimedia capabilities. You'll also learn about the different types of video and animation files often seen on the Internet.

Setting Up Your Video Display

When you installed Windows 95, it should have updated your system files to include any multimedia hardware drivers necessary to play sound and video files.

If you've added new multimedia hardware to your computer since you've installed Windows 95, it will have been detected automatically. For this reason, you won't have to do any hardware configuration of your system to get Internet Explorer to play sound and video files.

If your computer doesn't have at least 256-color capability, you may want to consider asking a computer retailer in your area for pricing on better hardware. Chances are, though, that you have hardware capable of supporting 256 colors. Just to be sure, though, here's a good way to check:

1. Click your right mouse button on your Desktop.
2. In the small menu that appears, select the Properties command. You will see the Display Properties dialog box.

3. At the top of the dialog box, click the Settings tab. Your screen will resemble the one in Figure 20.1.

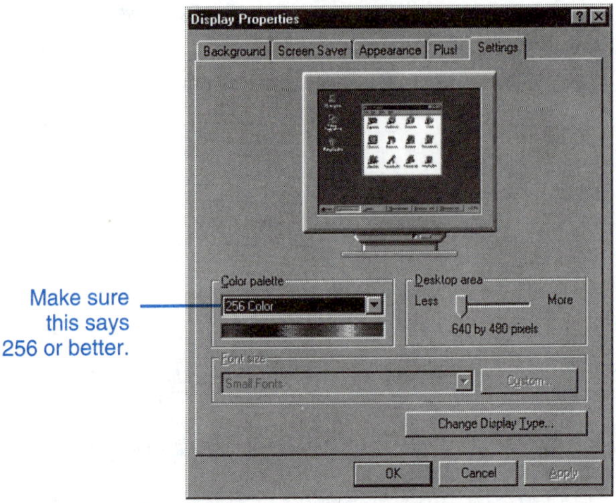

FIGURE 20.1 The Display Properties dialog box.

4. Underneath the Color palette, the color resolution of your adapter will be indicated. 256-color or higher is highly recommended.

If you don't have 256-color resolution, you may consider consulting your computer retailer for information on how to upgrade.

You'll also need to tell Windows 95 how to put video and animation on your screen. Since video is very complicated for a computer to do, there are certain things you'll want to configure to make the video appear smooth and seamless; otherwise, the video can be annoying to watch. Luckily, this configuration is a simple process.

To configure video and animation playback for Windows 95:

1. Open the Start menu on your Taskbar. You will see the main Start menu.

2. Open the Settings menu and select Control Panel. The Control Panel window will appear.
3. Double-click the Multimedia icon. You'll see the Multimedia Properties dialog.
4. Click the Video tab at the top of the dialog box. Your window will resemble the one shown in Figure 20.2.

Use Original size for 386 or 486 computers.

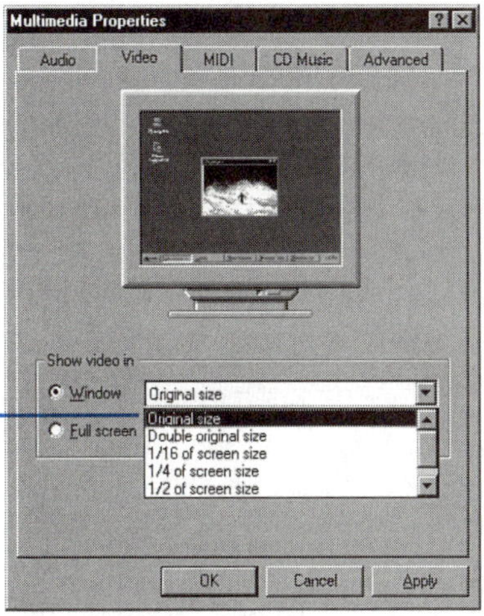

FIGURE 20.2 Video settings.

5. In the section labeled Show video in, you can tell Windows how large you want the video window to be. If you have a 386 or 486 processor, it is best to leave this at Original size. If you have a Pentium, you can set this to Double original size.

I usually use one of these two settings, but feel free to experiment.

LEARNING VIDEO FILE EXTENSIONS

As with sound files, video and animation files come in a variety of formats. Each format is designed to fit a particular purpose, and each one has its place. Although, for the most part, the type of file isn't important, there are some things you'll want to keep in mind as you surf through multimedia cyberspace:

- .AVI The Windows 95 Media Player has built-in support for .AVI files. You won't need to configure anything for these to work.
- .MPG Windows has no viewer for these files. Although you can download viewers from the Internet, you'll have to configure them yourself.
- .MOV Windows has no viewer for these files, either. You'll have to download a copy of QuickTime for Windows (use Yahoo to search for it). Unfortunately, these files only work if they are specially prepared by the user who put them on the Internet. Otherwise, you'll only get them to work with a Macintosh, not a Windows 95 PC.
- .FLI The Windows 95 Media Player has built-in support for .FLI files, too. You won't need to configure anything for these to work.

If you want to play .AVI files, you won't need to configure a thing. Windows 95 will play them automatically. Although you can get Window 95 viewers for .MOV files, the process is very difficult, and won't be discussed here. Not to mention, most of the .MOV files I've seen on the Internet are still in Macintosh format and can't be viewed anyway.

If you'd like to view .MPG files on the Internet, consider reading Que's *Special Edition Using Windows 95*.

Playing Video from the Internet

Internet Explorer has no built-in support for video or animation. If you choose to retrieve a file of this type, Internet Explorer will run another application to play the file. As with Web pages, gopher menus, sound files, and all the rest, you'll often see video files as a standard shortcut or hyperlink in the document. The context of the document should indicate that you'll be retrieving a video file.

> **These Take Forever!** Since video files are usually quite large, you should be prepared to wait several minutes for a file to come through. Some files can take an hour or more to transfer, especially if you're accessing the Internet over a modem.

For an example, I'll take you out to the Los Almos National Laboratory for a unique look at our solar system. The file I use for the example is about 1 megabyte in size, so you'll want to be prepared to wait between 60 seconds and 15 minutes (depending on the speed of your system). If you get tired of waiting for the file, you can always use the Stop button on the toolbar to cancel the transfer. You should still get a good understanding of how this works.

1. Open the File menu and select the Open command. You'll see the Open Internet Address dialog box.
2. Type **http://www.c3.lanl.gov/~cjhamil/SolarSystem** and press Enter. *Be sure to capitalize it the same way I did.* After a few moments, you'll see the Views of the Solar System page, as shown in Figure 20.3.
3. Use the scroll bar or down arrow to browse down the page until you see a list of the planets in our solar system, as shown in Figure 20.4.

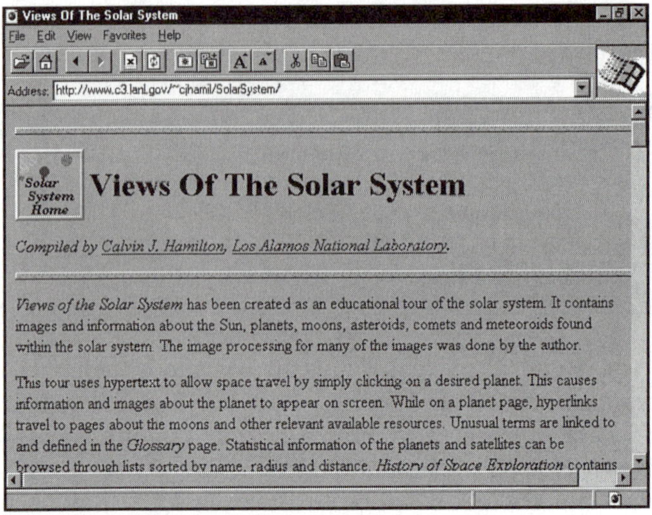

FIGURE 20.3 The Views of the Solar System page.

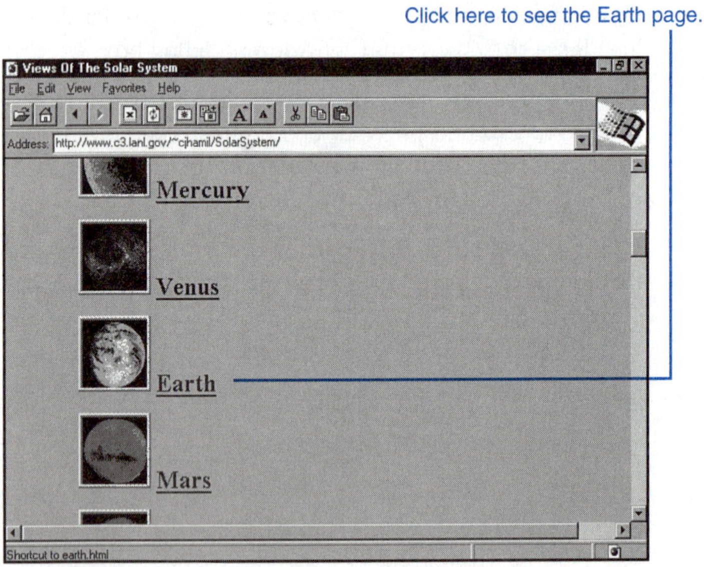

FIGURE 20.4 A list of the planets.

4. Click the Earth shortcut. After a few moments, you'll see the Earth page, as shown in Figure 20.5.

Click here to see the Earth Movies.

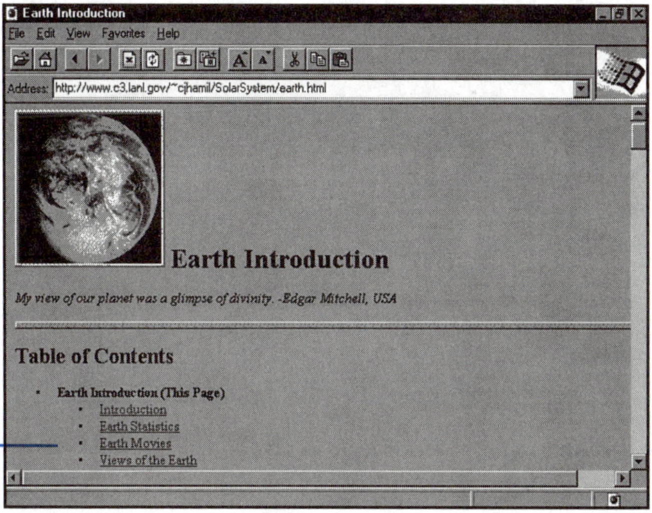

FIGURE 20.5 The Earth page.

5. In the outline of subjects, click the Earth Movies shortcut. You'll see a list of video clips about the Earth, as shown in Figure 20.6.

6. In the list of Earth Movies, click the AVI shortcut next to Earth/Venus Rotation Movie. After about 2 to 15 minutes, the video will play on your screen.

Click here to view the Earth/Venus Rotation video clip.

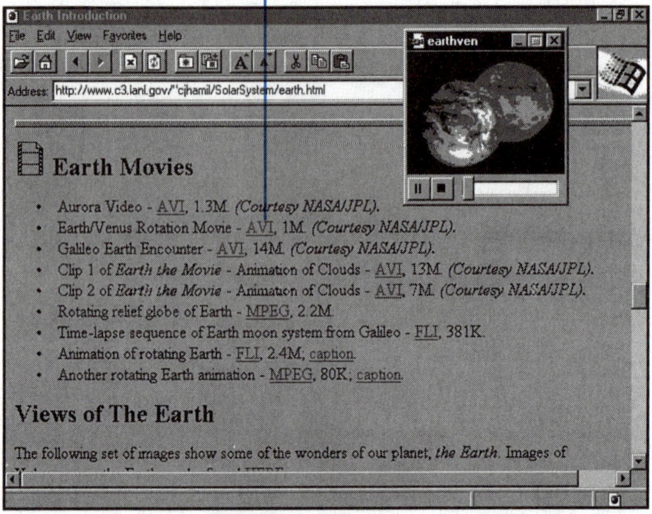

FIGURE 20.6 A list of Earth video clips.

> **I Missed It!** Uh-oh! After all that time, you missed it. You went to get a soda, and when you came back, the video had already played. Don't worry, it's still on your hard drive, and you can still see it if you want to. Open the Start menu, select Find Files or Folders, click the Advanced tab, and choose File of Type Video Clip. Click Find Now to locate the files on your machine. After a few moments, you should see earthgal in the list at the bottom. Double-click it to see it again.

In this lesson, you learned how to configure Internet Explorer to play video and animation files, if your machine has multimedia capabilities. You also learned about the different types of video and animation files often seen on the Internet.

In the next lesson, you'll learn how to configure the advanced and technical options of Internet Explorer.

Configuring Advanced Options

Lesson 21

In this lesson, you'll learn how to configure the advanced and technical options of Internet Explorer. This lesson includes information about the Start Page, the History folder, and the Document Cache.

Choosing Your Start Page

When you first start Internet Explorer, you see the Microsoft home page. Internet Explorer is set, at first, to bring up this page whenever you start it. That's why we call it the Start Page. If you want, you can change it.

While changing the Start Page is easy, deciding on a *good* Start Page is something else entirely. It's important to make your Start Page something you'll use frequently. When choosing a Start Page, consider the following points:

- The Start Page will appear every time you start Internet Explorer. If you use a page frequently, this is a good candidate for a Start Page.
- Many people (including myself) will use a search engine for a Start Page. I use the Yahoo search page. If you'd like to use a different one, you can.
- Some people choose a page with news about the industry in which they work. This way, the first thing they see in the morning is a complete update on the happenings of the industry. This, of course, is very handy, and can offer you a distinct competitive edge in your field.

If you've chosen a Start Page, you can use it instead of the one I use in the example in the next section.

SETTING YOUR START PAGE

After you've chosen your Start Page, you need to tell Internet Explorer to use it from now on. I'll use the Yahoo search page as an example, but you can use a different one, if you'd like.

1. Open the File menu and select the Open command. You will see the Open Internet Address dialog box.
2. Type **http://www.yahoo.com/search.html** and press Enter. After a few moments, you will see the Yahoo search page.
3. Open the View menu and select the Options command. You will see the Options dialog box.
4. Click the Start Page tab at the top of the dialog box. You will see the Start Page options, as shown in Figure 21.1.

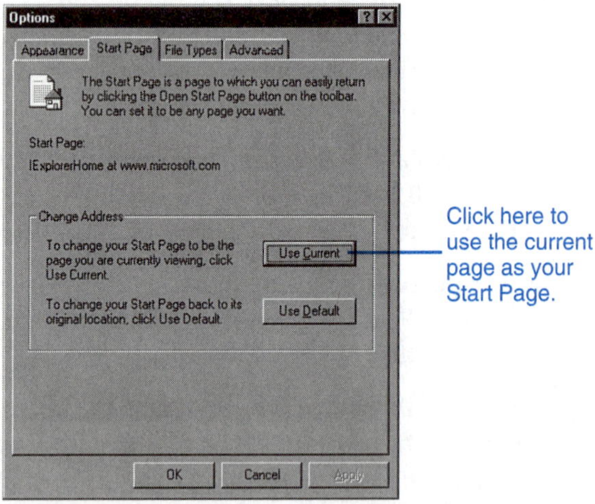

FIGURE 21.1 The Start Page options.

5. To set the current page as your Start Page, click the Use Current button.
6. If you change your mind later, you can click the Use Default button to set the Start Page back to the Microsoft home page.

Any time you want to change the Start Page, follow the steps I've outlined above, using your own URL instead of the Yahoo search URL.

Configuring the History Folder

Although I've covered a few of these items in previous lessons, I'm including everything here so that this serves as a better reference for you.

Internet Explorer allows you to do three things with the History folder:

- Specify the number of documents to be kept in the History folder
- Change the location of the History folder
- Empty the History folder

Setting the Maximum Number of Documents

From time to time, you may notice that the History folder contains either more documents than you wish to sift through, or maybe you'd like the History folder to contain more documents than it does.

If you don't browse the Web very often, you'll find that the History folder can fill up with every document you've ever visited. This can make it very difficult to find a document, since there would be so many. Or, perhaps you'd like to conserve hard disk space. Who knows?

You might have reason to want to save more files in the History folder. I like to keep a lot of them in there. It seems like no matter how unimportant a Web document seems to be, someone will ask, "Have you seen any information about..." and I'll say, "Yes, but I don't remember where." Now that I can save all that information, I can go back through the History folder and find that information for the other person. The more documents I keep, the more valuable the list becomes, but the more complicated it can become.

To specify the maximum number of documents the History folder will contain:

1. If you already see the Options dialog box, skip to step 3. Otherwise...
2. Open the View menu and select the Options command. You will see the Options dialog box.
3. Click the Advanced tab at the top of the Options dialog box. You will see the Advanced options, as shown in Figure 21.2.

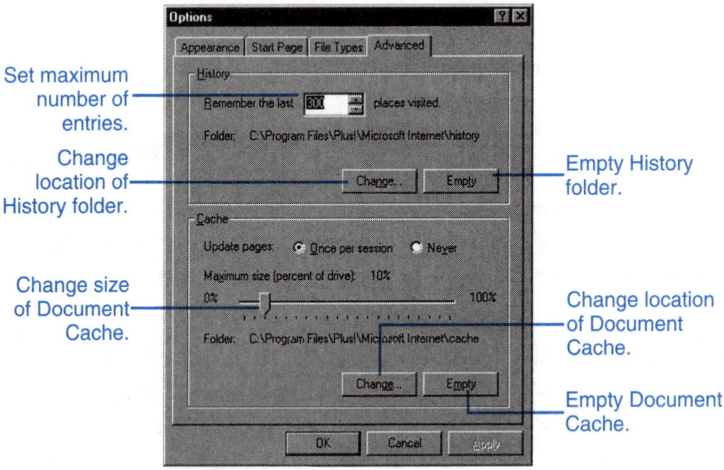

FIGURE 21.2 The Advanced options.

4. In the box labeled History, you'll see **Remember the last 300 places visited**. Use the spin controls to increase or decrease the number. Or, you can type a specific number. The range is 0–3000. If you don't want to use the History folder at all, set this value to 0.

CHANGING THE LOCATION OF THE HISTORY FOLDER

By default, Internet Explorer will place these History files in a folder on your hard drive. The default path is C:\Program Files\Plus!\Microsoft Internet\history. In most cases, this location will work fine.

You may, though, want to change the location of the History folder. For example, I keep all of my customized data on a second hard disk. I'd rather the History folder be there, too.

To change the location of the History folder:

1. If you already see the Options dialog box, skip to step 3. Otherwise...
2. Open the View menu and select the Options command. You will see the Options dialog box.
3. Click the Advanced tab at the top of the screen (if you've been following through this entire lesson, you're already there). You will see the Advanced options as shown in Figure 21.2.
4. In the box labeled History, make a note of the current location of the History folder. You'll find the information in the middle of the box. It's labeled Folder:.
5. To change the location, click the Change button. You will see the Browse for Folder dialog box as shown in Figure 21.3.
6. Select the folder in which you'd like to store your History files.

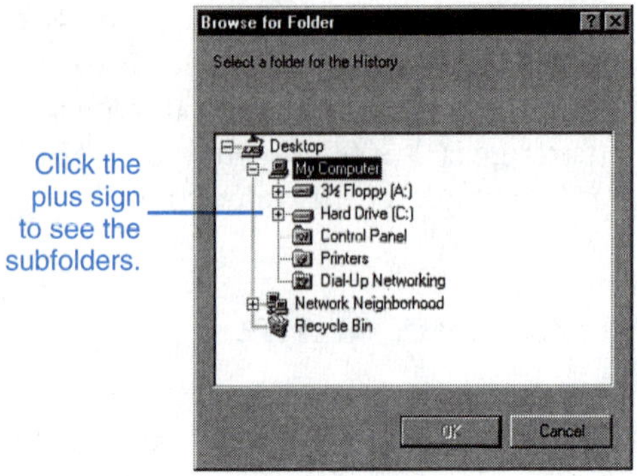

FIGURE 21.3 The Browse for Folder dialog box.

EMPTYING THE HISTORY FOLDER

I can pretty much promise you that, at one point or another, your History folder will become filled with useless information, and you'll want to empty it.

To empty the History folder:

1. If you already see the Options dialog box, skip to step 3. Otherwise...
2. Open the View menu and select the Options command. You will see the Options dialog box.
3. Click the Advanced tab at the top of the screen (if you've been following through this entire lesson, you're already there). You will see the Advanced options, as shown in Figure 21.2.
4. In the box labeled History, click the Empty button. You will see the Empty Folder dialog box asking you if you're sure you want to empty the History folder.
5. If you're sure, click Yes to empty the folder. If you change your mind, click No.

CONFIGURING THE DOCUMENT CACHE

Internet Explorer uses a Document Cache to prevent constant access to the Internet for information you already have. For example, if a graphic is used at the top of every page at a certain Web site, there is no reason to download the graphic every time. You can save the graphic to the hard disk, and if you ever need to use it again, it's already handy.

The Document Cache also improves the speed with which you can browse the Web. If you decide to use the Back arrow to go back to the previous page, Internet Explorer simply reads that previous page from the hard disk instead of retrieving it from the hard disk.

By default, Internet Explorer will check for each graphic and page once every time you use Internet Explorer. After that, it will assume that you have a current version. So, if you frequently start Internet Explorer and then shut it down again, you'll never get to take advantage of the Document Cache.

To avoid this problem, you can tell Internet Explorer not to update the pages. To do this:

1. If you already see the Options dialog box, skip to step 3. Otherwise...
2. Open the View menu and select the Options command. You will see the Options dialog box.
3. Click the Advanced tab at the top of the screen (if you've been following through this entire lesson, you're already there). You will see the Advanced options, as shown in Figure 21.2.
4. In the box labeled Cache, click the radio button labeled Never (next to Update pages).

My Documents Are Still Old! If you've told Internet Explorer never to update the documents, you'll never see newer versions of Web pages as they are updated at the other end. To see a current version (if you think it's been updated), click the Refresh button on your toolbar.

Changing the Size of the Document Cache

By default, Internet Explorer will use a maximum of 10 percent of your total hard disk space to store Web pages and graphics. If you want to use more or less, you can specify a percentage, but you can't specify a specific amount of space. To increase or decrease the size of your Document Cache:

1. If you already see the Options dialog box, skip to step 3. Otherwise...
2. Open the View menu and select the Options command. You will see the Options dialog box.
3. Click the Advanced tab at the top of the screen (if you've been following through this entire lesson, you're already there). You will see the Advanced options, as shown in Figure 21.2.
4. In the box labeled Cache, move the slider underneath Maximum size with your mouse.

Changing the Location of the Document Cache

By default, Internet Explorer will place the Document Cache in a folder on your hard drive. The default path is C:\Program Files\Plus!\Microsoft Internet\Cache. In most cases, this location will work fine.

You may, though, want to change this location. To change the location of the Document Cache:

1. If you already see the Options dialog box, skip to step 3. Otherwise...
2. Open the View menu and select the Options command. You will see the Options dialog box.
3. Click the Advanced tab at the top of the screen (if you've been following through this entire lesson, you're already there). You will see the Advanced options, as shown in Figure 21.2.
4. In the box labeled Cache, make a note of the current location of the Cache. You'll find the information in the middle of the box. It's labeled Folder:.
5. To change the location, click the Change button. You will see the Browse for Folder dialog box as shown in Figure 21.3.
6. In the window, select from the list the folders in which you'd like to store your Document Cache.

EMPTYING THE DOCUMENT CACHE

If you find that the Document Cache is taking up too much room on your hard drive, you can delete all the information and start over.

To empty the Document Cache:

1. If you already see the Options dialog box, skip to step 3. Otherwise...
2. Open the View menu and select the Options command. You will see the Options dialog box.
3. Click the Advanced tab at the top of the screen (if you've been following through this entire lesson, you're already there). You will see the Advanced options, as shown in Figure 21.2.

4. In the box labeled Cache, click the Empty button. You will see the Empty Folder dialog box asking you if you're sure you want to empty the Document Cache.
5. If you're sure, click Yes to empty the folder. If you change your mind, click No.

In this lesson, you learned how to configure the advanced and technical options of Internet Explorer.

In the appendixes at the end of this book, I'll show you some cool Web sites and help you install Internet Explorer on your machine (if you haven't already).

Interesting Web Sites

APPENDIX A

I've been using the World Wide Web for quite some time, and I've found a number of different sites that contain useful, interesting, or entertaining information. I've included a list of some of them here.

Each entry starts with the URL. See Lesson 1 for more information about URLs. You can type **URL** into the Open URL dialog box in Internet Explorer. See Lesson 3 for more information on how to download a Web document (browse the Web) with Internet Explorer.

> **Watch for Capitalization!** In most cases, you'll need to type these URLs *exactly* as you see them here. This includes the correct uppercase and lowercase letters.

http://www.w3.org/hypertext/DataSources/Top.html A general overview of the Web. This is a great starting-points document for the beginning Web user. If you're new to Web browsing, start here.

http://arts.usf.edu The University of South Florida College of Fine Arts, with over 500 students, is home to the Art, Dance, and Theatre Departments, and the School of Music, as well as the USF Contemporary Art Museum and Graphic studio.

http://gallery.sjsu.edu This is the World Wide Web server for the Art Department at San Jose State University. You can find information about art shows and some interesting facts about new artists.

http://www.westga.edu/~coop This is JOBNET, a collection of job-related resources scattered across the Internet that have been collected from various sources. Sources used include gopher, Usenet News, and World Wide Web.

http://www.careermag.com/careermag The network world has career opportunities, whether you are changing positions or building contacts and ideas for the future. *Career Magazine* is a comprehensive resource, designed to meet the individual needs of networked job seekers. You can return to *Career Magazine* for valuable new information every day. Put *Career Magazine*'s URL into your Favorites document and begin your networked career search.

http://web.fie.com This is the Federal Information Exchange, facilitating a partnership of 10 federal agencies under the leadership of the Department of Energy. Today, Federal Information Exchange's FEDIX/MOLIS On-Line Information System has 125,000+ users. Be sure to check out FEDIX, which contains federal agency opportunity information.

http://www.pathfinder.com/pathfinder/Greet.html This is Time Warner. This page contains links to most of Time's publications, including: *TIME, Sports Illustrated, People, Money,* and others.

http://www.dbisna.com This is Dun and Bradstreet. You can find information on market research, management, and other financial topics.

http://www.tti.com This is Citibank, the largest and most innovative financial service provider in the United States.

http://meta.stanford.edu/quotes.html This is a killer collection of great one-liners.

http://www.brandonu.ca/~ennsnr/Tags Tag lines, more tag lines, and even more tag lines. There are currently over 50,000 tag lines in this collection.

http://www.msstate.edu/Movies The Internet Movie Database at Mississippi State University. Great for movie reviews and information on actors and actresses.

http://www.music.fsu.edu/ftp.html Music Instruction Software, Sounds, and Pictures, which also shows a nice example of using inline graphics as bullets for a list.

http://www.shopping2000.com:80/shopping2000/tower The Tower Records Home Page, which contains a link to a searchable database of the entire Tower Catalog. Great for gifts and that hard-to-find LP.

http://www.music.sony.com This is Sony online; a great page with lots of killer links, but very graphics-intensive. This page could take awhile to download with Internet Explorer.

http://webcrawler.cs.washington.edu/WebCrawler This is the WebCrawler I talked about in Lesson 10. The WebCrawler is one of the best searching tools available today.

http://www.att.net/dir800 This AT&T 800 Directory on the Internet is one more value-added service from your friends at AT&T. Keep this one in your Favorites folder, but remember to read the copyright notice.

http://www.microsoft.com The Microsoft Home Page, which contains great information about Microsoft's upcoming products, including Windows 95. You'll even find Microsoft employment opportunities.

http://www.compuserve.com CompuServe, of course. You'll find links to a CompuServe overview, CompuServe press releases, MultiMedia, and CompuServe Internet Services.

http://www.bsdi.com Berkeley Software Design, Inc., the makers of BSD UNIX. This is a great-looking Web page that demonstrates the effect of colorful lists. This page contains many links to tons of great information about the company plus current issues and discussions about the operating system.

http://www.intel.com The folks who made my Pentium. These pages are easily among the most attractive I've ever seen. Browse for current press releases and information on Intel products. Notice the carefully placed graphics and subtle shading.

http://www.creaf.com Creative Labs, Inc., based in Milpitas, California, is the leader in PC sound, video, and CD-ROM multimedia solutions with Sound Blaster setting the industry standard for sound on PC-based platforms. Creative Labs, Inc. develops, manufactures, and markets a family of multimedia sound and video products and a range of multimedia kits for entertainment, education, and productivity markets. This Web page provides information about Creative's product line.

http://www.sprintlink.net SprintLink is a commercial Internet service provider; this site offers information about current products and services.

http://www.netscape.com This is Netscape Communications, Inc., makers of the Netscape Web browser, and NetSite Web server. Arguably, Netscape is the finest Internet technology available to the consumer today. If you're looking for a Web browser, this is the place to go.

http://www.sun.com This is the home page for Sun Microsystems, makers of UNIX Workstations, Solaris, and much more. Check out the Technology & Research link for some very interesting information.

http://www.cray.com This is Cray Research. They make incredibly powerful computers that cost several million dollars a piece. Find out more about the leading edge of supercomputing technology as well. See figure A.1.

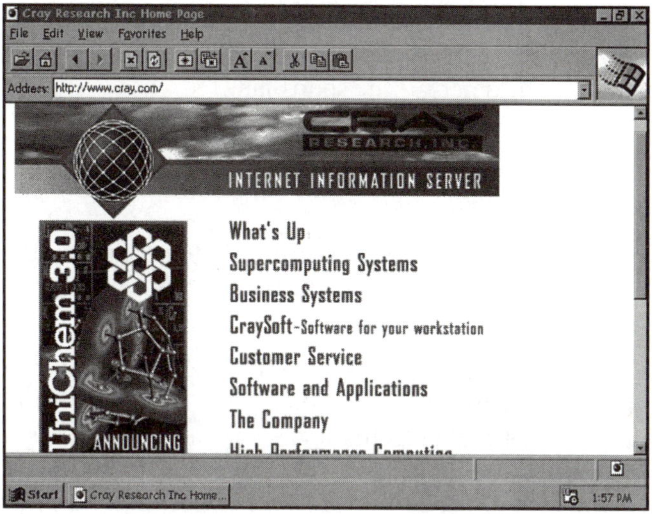

FIGURE A.1 The Cray Research home page.

http://www.ibm.com/ I'm sure you've heard of these folks. They're IBM. Get information about IBM's market performance and new product releases.

http://www.apple.com Downloading this page may take awhile. The graphics are quite large, and there are a lot of them. This Web page contains many great images and tons of information about Apple and Apple products.

http://www.dell.com Dell Computer Corporation designs, develops, manufactures, markets, services, and supports a complete line of personal computers compatible with industry standards. This page is also rather graphics-intensive. You'll find information on Dell's extensive product line.

http://www.xerox.com A very extensive online database of Xerox information, from product announcements to press releases to link to XSoft, the software division of Xerox.

http://www.vegas.com It's all here. Great information about the town including tips on how to spend lots of money! No bets online, though.

http://tns-www.lcs.mit.edu/cgi-bin/sports Up-to-date and complete coverage of your favorite teams and sports issues. A must for the Internet-surfing sports fan.

http://www.tvnet.com/UTVL/utvl.html This page contains links to hundreds of pages concerning hundreds of popular TV shows, past and present.

http://www.cgl.com/~it Use this URL to get information about international flights, domestic flights, tours, cruises, and travel news.

http://www.commerce.net CommerceNet is a not-for-profit mutual benefit corporation that is conducting the first large-scale market trial of technologies and business processes to support electronic commerce via the Internet. You can find all kinds of information about the prospect of electronic commerce via the Internet.

http://www.directory.net A directory of commercial services, products, and information available on the Internet.

https://www.internet.net The Internet Shopping Network. You can join the ISN and shop for products and services via the Internet.

http://www.quote.com Quote.Com is a service dedicated to providing quality financial market data to the Internet community. This includes current quotes on stocks, commodity futures, mutual funds, and bonds. It also includes business news, market analysis and commentary, fundamental (balance sheet) data, and company profiles.

http://www.acm.uiuc.edu/rml/govt.html This page contains links to the major branches of the United States government and loads of information about each one.

http://branch.com Branch Mall. A shopping mall on the Internet. Use this URL to access tons of information and thousands of vendors on the Internet.

http://www.comdex.com:8000 COMDEX, a computer convention, maintains this page. Use it to get information about upcoming COMDEX events or to register for the show.

http://www.yellow.com The World Wide Yellow Pages. Use this URL to search for countless vendors, service providers, and news resources on the Internet.

http://www.ncsa.uiuc.edu/SDG/Software/Mosaic/Docs/whats-new.html What's new on the Web. This constantly changing page, courtesy of NCSA, contains links to new resources and information that affects many Internet users. Consult this URL weekly.

http://www.mcp.com This is Macmillan's home page. They are the people who bring you this book as well as most of the best computer books in the world. Check this site frequently for up-to-date information about the availability of books on the topics you wish to explore. See figure A.2.

FIGURE A.2 The Macmillan home page.

http://www.well.com/user/caferace/vrml.html This site contains tons of great information about VRML, the **V**irtual **R**eality **M**odeling **L**anguage. VRML, although still a young technology, will undoubtedly become a major force in World Wide Web technology over the next couple of years. Browse through the links; they're very interesting.

Appendix B

Where Can I Get Internet Explorer?

In this appendix, I'll explain how to get a copy of Internet Explorer.

From the Microsoft Plus! Companion

In addition to Windows 95, Microsoft has released the Microsoft Plus! Companion for Windows 95. With Plus!, you get:

- Visual enhancements for faster, more powerful machines.
- Internet Jumpstart Kit. This includes Internet Explorer and an Internet mail service for Microsoft Exchange.
- Desktop Themes. A collection of graphics, sounds and screen savers to change the look of your PC.
- Much more...

Since I'm not here to advertise Plus! (although I highly recommend it), we'll stick to the Internet Jumpstart Kit.

Microsoft plans to release a copy of Plus! with every copy of Windows 95, but only for a brief introductory period of time. After that, you'll have to buy a copy of Plus!. If you didn't get the free copy, don't worry. It won't cost very much, and it's well worth the money.

In the next appendix, I'll show you how to install Internet Explorer from the Plus! Companion.

FROM MSN: THE MICROSOFT NETWORK

If you join MSN (The Microsoft Network), MSN will automatically prompt you for installing a copy of Internet Explorer on your machine. Although I can't be sure exactly how this will work (since MSN wasn't ready when I wrote this), it's supposed to go something like this:

After you join MSN, you'll see an e-mail message in your Inbox. This message will give you step-by-step instructions on exactly what to do to get a copy of Internet Explorer. And, you're in luck. Not only will MSN send you a copy of Internet Explorer over the Internet, it will actually install it for you. You won't have to worry about a thing. All the settings are configured for you after you answer a few simple questions.

OK, here's a way to get Internet Explorer for free if you already use a different Internet Service Provider (so you don't need access through MSN) and you don't want to pay for the Plus! Companion:

1. Join MSN. Double-click the icon on your Desktop and follow the instructions.
2. Follow the instructions in the e-mail I told you about.
3. Cancel your subscription to MSN.

Keep in mind, though, if you install Internet Explorer without Plus!, you won't have access to several key tools that make working with the Internet easier (like the Internet mail client and the Dialup Scripting Tool). For more information how to use the Internet effectively and productively with Windows 95, consider reading Que's *The 10 Minute Guide to Using the Internet with Windows 95*.

Installing Internet Explorer

APPENDIX C

In this appendix, I give you step-by-step instructions for installing Internet Explorer from the Microsoft Plus! Companion for Windows 95.

Starting the Setup Program

If you're using the CD-ROM version, place the CD into your CD-ROM drive. If you're installing from floppy disks, place the first disk in your floppy drive.

To start the Setup program:

1. Click the Start menu button on your taskbar. You will see the main Start menu.
2. Open the Settings group and select the Control Panel command. You will see the Control Panel window.
3. Double-click the Add/Remove Programs icon. You'll see the Add/Remove Programs Properties dialog box as shown in Figure C.1.
4. Click the Install button. You'll see the Install Program dialog box, as shown in Figure C.2.
5. Click the Next button. Windows 95 will search your system for a setup program and find it. You will then see the Run Installation Program dialog box, as shown in Figure C.3.

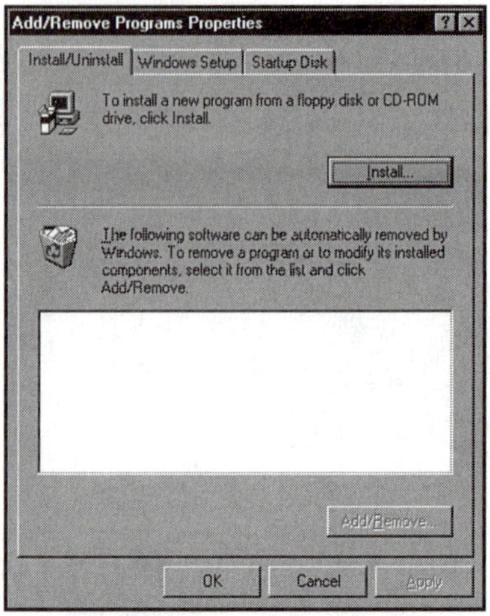

FIGURE C.1 The Add/Remove Programs Properties dialog box.

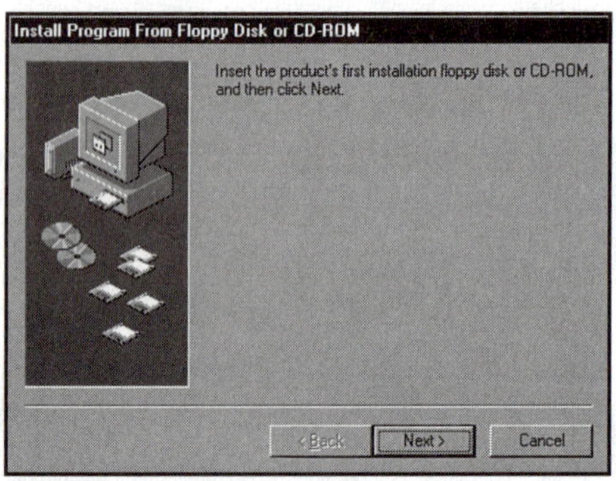

FIGURE C.2 The Install Program dialog box.

> **Watch Out for Floppies!** If you're installing Internet Explorer from a CD-ROM disk, make sure there are no disks in your floppy drives, since Windows 95 will search the floppy drives first. You may start to setup the wrong program if the floppy disk contains an installation program.

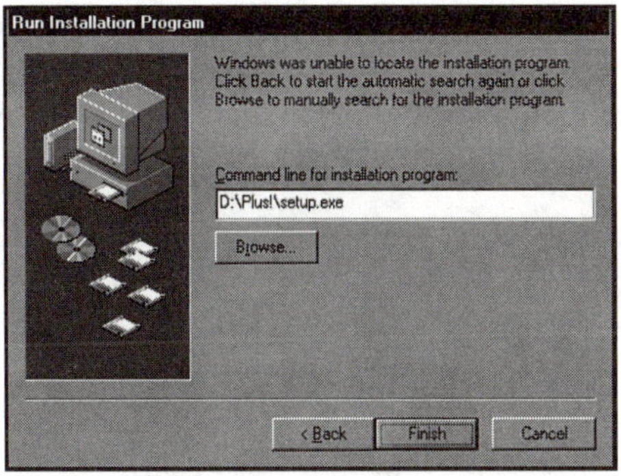

FIGURE C.3 The Run Installation Program dialog box.

6. To begin the installation, click the Finish button. The Microsoft Setup program will start. After a few minutes, you'll see the main Setup dialog.
7. Click the Continue button. You'll see the Name and Organization Information dialog box.
8. Type the appropriate information (if it's not already there), and click OK. You should see a confirmation dialog that wants to know if you've typed the information correctly. If you did, click OK. If you didn't, click Change and repeat this step.
9. You will see a dialog box that gives you a product number. Write this number down on your registration card before you send it in. After you've written the number down, click OK.
10. The next dialog box that appears wants to know where you want Plus! to be installed. Usually, the default will work fine. If you want to change it, click the Change Folder button and specify a new location (if the directory doesn't exist, the setup program will create if for you). After you've changed the folder (or decided to keep the default), click OK.

11. Setup will search your hard drive for a previous copy of Plus! (not very likely that you'll have one). After a few moments, you'll see the Setup dialog box shown in Figure C.4.

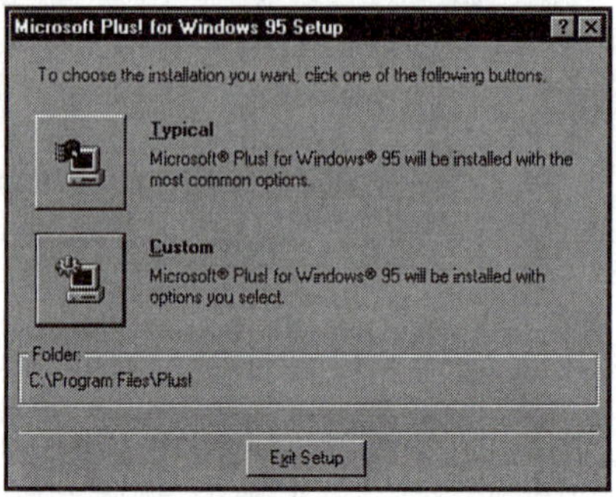

Figure C.4 The Setup dialog box.

12. Although I'd normally tell to you choose Typical, I'd recommend using the Custom install on this one. Some of the default options use a LOT of hard disk space, and you might not want them. Click the Custom button to continue.

13. You should see the Custom dialog box. I can't really give you too much advice on what to choose here, but you'll want to make sure that Internet Jumpstart Kit is checked (see Figure C.5). If you're interested in saving some hard disk space, you can remove the check from Desktop Themes (about 16 Megabytes of sounds, graphics, icons, screen savers, and other multimedia fun stuff). Some of the options (such as Desktop Themes) also have suboptions that you can configure. To install only some of the Desktop Themes, click the Change button. After you've made your choices, click the Continue button.

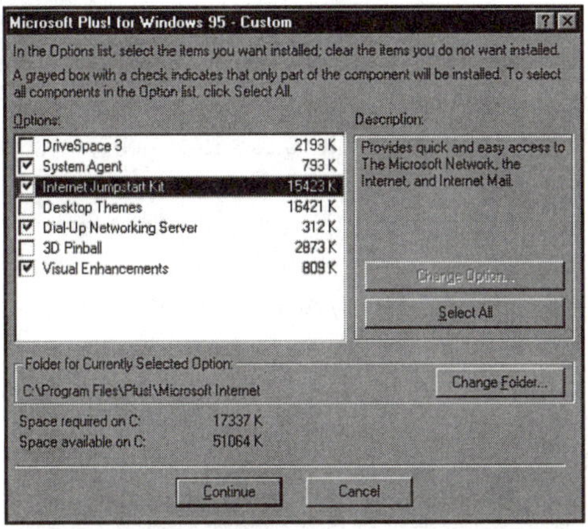

FIGURE C.5 The Custom Installation dialog box.

14. Setup will check for necessary disk space and then begin to copy files to your hard disk. If you're using a CD-ROM, you won't need to bother with it for a few moments. If you're using floppy disks, you'll need to change the disks as it prompts you. After that process is complete, you'll see the Internet Setup Wizard, as shown in Figure C.6.

FIGURE C.6 The Internet Setup Wizard.

15. To begin the Internet Setup process, click the Next button. Since step-by-step instructions are provided with the Internet Setup Wizard, I'll let you follow those and meet you at the end. Refer back to me here when you see the dialog box in Figure C.7. If you're ever not sure which option to choose, select the default of the one labeled recommended. If you're really stumped, contact your Internet Service Provider, or read Que's *Using Microsoft Internet Explorer* for answers to your questions.

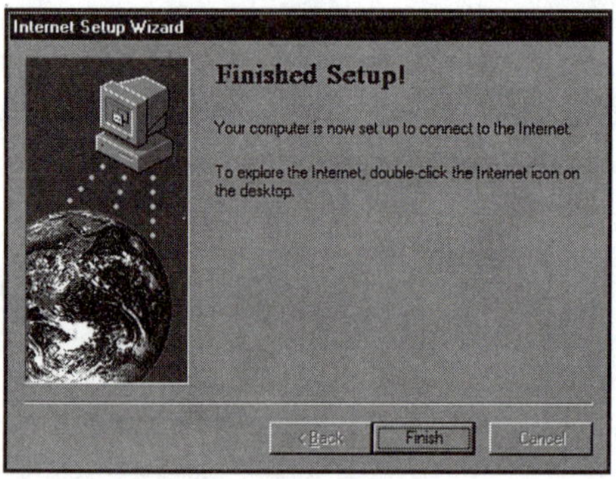

FIGURE C.7 You're finished!

16. After you've finished with the Internet Setup Wizard and the Install process, you'll be asked to restart Windows 95. Click the Restart button.

17. After Windows 95 restarts, you'll be ready to go! Jump in to Lesson 1 to see how to get started.

Adding New File Types

Appendix D

In this appendix, you'll learn how to add new file types to the Windows 95 registry.

Why Do I Need to Add File Types?

In order for Internet Explorer to display video files or play sound files correctly, you must have a viewer installed for each type of file. Lessons 19 and 20 show you which file types are supported by Internet Explorer, but if you'd like to view other types of files, like Quick Time movies or MPEG movies, you'll have to install a separate program that can display them for you.

If you install a true Windows 95 application, you won't need to add a file type. However, many freeware and shareware programs do not perform this step automatically. Therefore, you'll have to add a file type so Internet Explorer knows how to display it for you.

The most common application users of Internet Explorer will need is an MPEG movie player. There are a lot of them out there. If you need one, browse to **http://www.yahoo.com** and do a search on **MPEG movie player**. You should find a bunch of them.

After you've installed the program, see if you can view MPEG files (or whatever files you're trying to view). If you can, then you're all set. If not, you'll need to manually add a file type. The next section shows you how.

Adding File Types to the Registry

To add a new file type:

1. Open the View menu and select the Options command. You will see the Options dialog box.
2. Click the File Types tab at the top of the dialog box. You will see the File Types Options, as shown in Figure D.1.

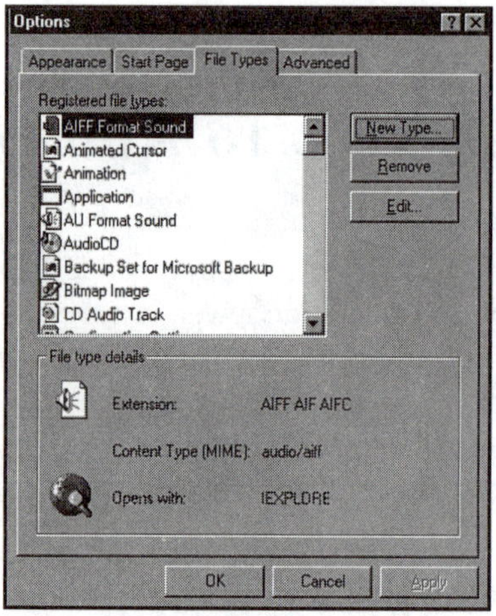

Figure D.1 The File Types Options.

3. The list in the window is a list of all the current file types for your system. To add a new file type, click the New Type button. You will see the Add New File Type dialog box, as shown in Figure D.2.
4. In the box labeled Description:, type a description for your new file type. If you're adding a file type for .MPG files, type in something like **MPEG Movie**.

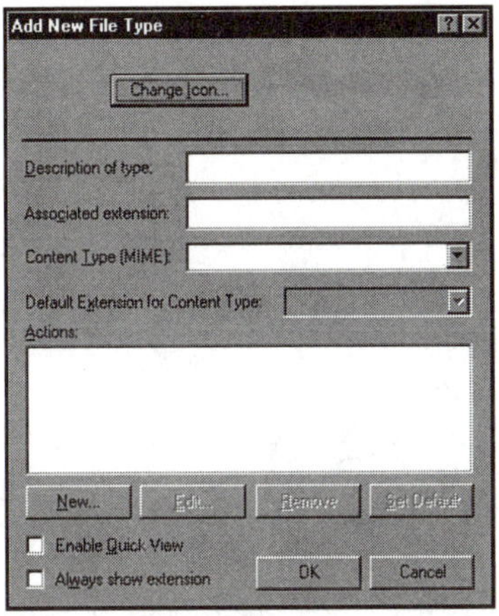

Figure D.2 Adding a new file type.

5. In the box labeled Associated Extension:, type the extension for the new file type. If you're adding a file type for .MPG files, type **MPG**. If you see an error message telling you the extension is already in use, then the file type has already been registered; you don't need to go any further. To get back out, click the **Cancel** button in each of the dialog boxes.

> **I Got the Error Message, But I Still Can't View MPEG Movie Files.** The .mpg extension may be associated with the wrong program. To check this, go back into View, Options, File Types. Under Registered file types, scroll down the list until you find an .mpg extension shown under File type details. Look at the Opens With label. If it is not your MPEG application, choose Edit (file type) and then Edit (action). Type in or browse for the correct program under Application used to perform action.

6. In the box labeled Content Type (MIME):, type the MIME information for the specific file type. If you're adding a

file type for .MPG files, this field should read **video/ mpg**. If you're adding a different file type, the Content Type must consist of the registered MIME for that particular kind of file.

> **MIME**, which stands for Multi-purpose Internet Mail Extension, consists of two parts separated by a forward slash. The first part is called the MIME Type, and can be thought of as the general category of the file. The common MIME Types are text, image, video, audio, or application. The second part is called the MIME Subtype, and is the name of the new format. For more detailed information on MIME, consult Que's *Using Microsoft Internet Explorer*.

7. Toward the bottom of the dialog box, you see an empty list of actions. Underneath, click the New button. You will see the New Action dialog box, as shown in Figure D.3.

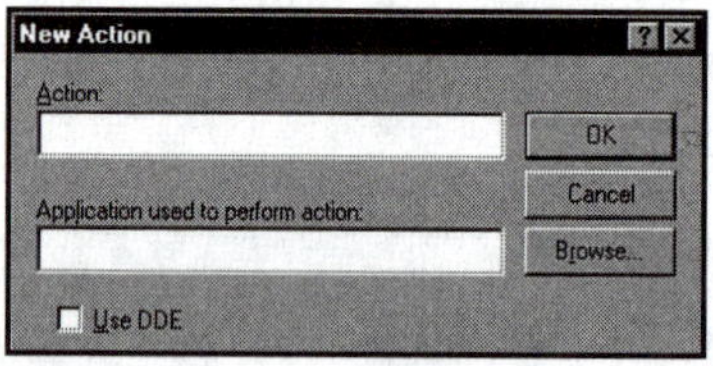

FIGURE D.3 Adding a new action.

8. In the box labeled Action:, type a name for the action. In most cases, just use Open.

9. In the box labeled Application used to perform action:, type the path and filename of the application used to display the file type. In the case of .MPG files, use the path and filename of your MPEG movie viewer. If you're not sure of the exact path or filename, click the Browse button.

10. Click OK to save your changes. The New Action dialog will disappear, and you'll go back to the Add New File Type dialog. Notice that the Actions list now contains Open.
11. Click the Change Icon button. You will see the Change Icon dialog box, as shown in Figure D.4.

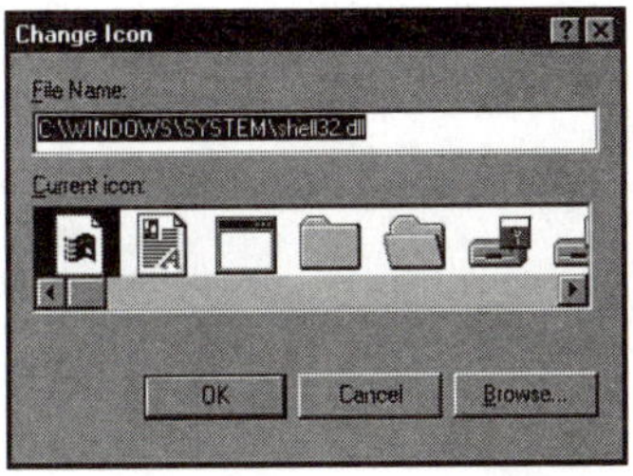

FIGURE D.4 Changing the icon.

12. Click the Browse button. You will see a second Change Icon dialog box. Use the browse window to find the application that displays your file type. In the case of .MPG files, find your MPEG movie viewer. After you've selected the file, you should see the icon for that program.
13. Double-click the icon. This will cause each data file (.MPG file, if that's what you're adding) to show this icon in your file lists.
14. To save your changes, click the OK button.

Many good MPEG files exist on the Internet; you should uncover some interesting sites in your Yahoo search. Florida State University has a healthy list at **http://euclid.math.fsu.edu/Art/art.html**.

INDEX

INDEX SECTION

A

B

C

D

E

F

G

H

I

J-K

L

M

Q-R

S

U

V

W

X–Y–Z

Complete and Return this Card for a *FREE* Computer Book Catalog

Thank you for purchasing this book! You have purchased a superior computer book written expressly for your needs. To continue to provide the kind of up-to-date, pertinent coverage you've come to expect from us, we need to hear from you. Please take a minute to complete and return this self-addressed, postage-paid form. In return, we'll send you a free catalog of all our computer books on topics ranging from word processing to programming and the internet.

Mr. ☐ Mrs. ☐ Ms. ☐ Dr. ☐

Name (first) ________ (M.I.) ☐ (last) ________

Address ________

____

City ________ State ____ Zip ________ ________

Phone ____ ____ ____ Fax ____ ____ ____

Company Name ________

E-mail address ________

1. Please check at least (3) influencing factors for purchasing this book.

- Front or back cover information on book .... ☐
- Special approach to the content .... ☐
- Completeness of content .... ☐
- Author's reputation .... ☐
- Publisher's reputation .... ☐
- Book cover design or layout .... ☐
- Index or table of contents of book .... ☐
- Price of book .... ☐
- Special effects, graphics, illustrations .... ☐
- Other (Please specify): ________ ☐

2. How did you first learn about this book?

- Internet Site .... ☐
- Saw in Macmillan Computer Publishing catalog .... ☐
- Recommended by store personnel .... ☐
- Saw the book on bookshelf at store .... ☐
- Recommended by a friend .... ☐
- Received advertisement in the mail .... ☐
- Saw an advertisement in: ________ ☐
- Read book review in: ________ ☐
- Other (Please specify): ________ ☐

3. How many computer books have you purchased in the last six months?

- This book only .... ☐
- 3 to 5 books .... ☐
- 2 books .... ☐
- More than 5 .... ☐

4. Where did you purchase this book?

- Bookstore .... ☐
- Computer Store .... ☐
- Consumer Electronics Store .... ☐
- Department Store .... ☐
- Office Club .... ☐
- Warehouse Club .... ☐
- Mail Order .... ☐
- Direct from Publisher .... ☐
- Internet site .... ☐
- Other (Please specify): .... ☐

5. How long have you been using a computer?

- Less than 6 months .. ☐
- 6 months to a year ..... ☐
- 1 to 3 years .... ☐
- More than 3 years ...... ☐

6. What is your level of experience with personal computers and with the subject of this book?

	With PC's	With subject of book
New	☐	☐
Casual	☐	☐
Accomplished	☐	☐
Expert	☐	☐

Source Code — ISBN: 0-7897-0628-8

7. Which of the following best describes your job title?

- Administrative Assistant ☐
- Coordinator ☐
- Manager/Supervisor ☐
- Director ☐
- Vice President ☐
- President/CEO/COO ☐
- Lawyer/Doctor/Medical Professional ☐
- Teacher/Educator/Trainer ☐
- Engineer/Technician ☐
- Consultant ☐
- Not employed/Student/Retired ☐
- Other (Please specify): ☐

8. Which of the following best describes the area of the company your job title falls under?

- Accounting ☐
- Engineering ☐
- Manufacturing ☐
- Marketing ☐
- Operations ☐
- Sales ☐
- Other (Please specify): ☐

9. What is your age?

- Under 20 ☐
- 21-29 ☐
- 30-39 ☐
- 40-49 ☐
- 50-59 ☐
- 60-over ☐

10. Are you:

- Male ☐
- Female ☐

11. Which computer publications do you read regularly? (Please list)

____

Comments: ______________________________

Fold here and scotch-tape to ma

NO POSTAGE NECESSARY IF MAILED IN THE UNITED STATES

BUSINESS REPLY MAIL
FIRST-CLASS MAIL PERMIT NO. 9918 INDIANAPOLIS IN

POSTAGE WILL BE PAID BY THE ADDRESSEE

ATTN MARKETING
MACMILLAN COMPUTER PUBLISHING
MACMILLAN PUBLISHING USA
201 W 103RD ST
INDIANAPOLIS IN 46209-9042